PRACTICAL SOCIAL WORK

Series Editor: Jo Campling

Social work is at an important stage in its development. All professions must be responsive to changing social and economic conditions if they are to meet the needs of those they serve. This series focuses on sound practice and the specific contributions which social workers can make to the well-being of our society.

The British Association of Social Workers has always been conscious of its role in setting guidelines for practice and in seeking to raise professional standards. The concept of the Practical Social Work series arose from a survey of BASW members to discover where they, the practitioners in social work, felt there was the most need for new literature. The response was overwhelming and enthusiastic, and the result is a carefully planned, coherent series of books. The emphasis is firmly on practice set in a theoretical framework. The books will inform, stimulate and promote discussion, thus adding to the further development of skills and high professional standards. All the authors are practitioners and teachers of social work, representing a wide variety of experience.

JO CAMPLING
A list of published titles in this series follows overleaf

Practical Social Work
Series Standing Order ISBN 0–333–69347–7
(*outside North America only*)

You can receive future titles in this series as they are published by placing a standing order. Please contact your bookseller or, in the case of difficulty, write to us at the address below with your name and address, the title of the series and the ISBN quoted above.

Customer Services Department, Palgrave Ltd
Houndmills, Basingstoke, Hampshire RG21 6XS, England

PRACTICAL SOCIAL WORK

Robert Adams *Social Work and Empowerment*

Sarah Banks *Ethics and Values in Social Work*

James G. Barber *Beyond Casework*

James G. Barber *Social Work with Addictions*

Peter Beresford and Suzy Croft *Citizen Involvement*

Suzy Braye and Michael Preston-Shoot *Practising Social Work Law (2nd edn)*

Helen Cosis Brown *Social Work and Sexuality*

Alan Butler and Colin Pritchard *Social Work and Mental Illness*

Crescy Cannan, Lynne Berry and Karen Lyons *Social Work and Europe*

Roger Clough *Residential Work*

David M. Cooper and David Ball *Social Work and Child Abuse*

Veronica Coulshed and Audrey Mullender *Management in Social Work (2nd edn)*

Veronica Coulshed and Joan Orme *Social Work Practice: An Introduction (3rd edn)*

Paul Daniel and John Wheeler *Social Work and Local Politics*

Peter R. Day *Sociology in Social Work Practice*

Lena Dominelli *Anti-Racist Social Work (2nd edn)*

Celia Doyle *Working with Abused Children (2nd edn)*

Angela Everitt and Pauline Hardiker *Evaluating for Good Practice*

Angela Everitt, Pauline Hardiker, Jane Littlewood and Audrey Mullender *Applied Research for Better Practice*

Kathy Ford and Alan Jones *Student Supervision*

David Francis and Paul Henderson *Working with Rural Communities*

Alison Froggatt *Family Work with Elderly People*

Danya Glaser and Stephen Frosh *Child Sexual Abuse (2nd edn)*

Gill Gorell Barnes *Working with Families*

Cordelia Grimwood and Ruth Popplestone *Women, Management and Care*

Jalna Hanmer and Daphne Statham *Women and Social Work (2nd edn)*

Tony Jeffs and Mark Smith (eds) *Youth Work*

Michael Kerfoot and Alan Butler *Problems of Childhood and Adolescence*

Joyce Lishman *Communication in Social Work*

Carol Lupton and Terry Gillespie (eds) *Working with Violence*

Mary Marshall and Mary Dixon *Social Work with Older People (3rd edn)*

Paula Nicolson and Rowan Bayne *Applied Psychology for Social Workers (2nd edn)*

Kieran O'Hagan *Crisis Intervention in Social Services*

Michael Oliver and Bob Sapey *Social Work with Disabled People (2nd edn)*

Joan Orme and Bryan Glastonbury *Care Management*

John Pitts *Working with Young Offenders*

Michael Preston-Shoot *Effective Groupwork*

Peter Raynor, David Smith and Maurice Vanstone *Effective Probation Practice*

Steven Shardlow and Mark Doel *Practice Learning and Teaching*

Carole R. Smith *Social Work with the Dying and Bereaved*

David Smith *Criminology for Social Work*

Christine Stones *Focus on Families*

Neil Thompson *Anti-Discriminatory Practice (3rd edn)*

Neil Thompson, Michael Murphy and Steve Stradling *Dealing with Stress*

Derek Tilbury *Working with Mental Illness*

Alan Twelvetrees *Community Work (2nd edn)*

Hilary Walker and Bill Beaumount (eds) *Working with Offenders*

Social Work with Disabled People

Second Edition

Michael Oliver
and
Bob Sapey

palgrave

First edition 1983
Reprinted seven times
Second edition 1999

Published by
PALGRAVE
Houndmills, Basingstoke, Hampshire RG21 6XS and
175 Fifth Avenue, New York, N.Y. 10010
Companies and representatives throughout the world

PALGRAVE is the new global academic imprint of
St. Martin's Press LLC Scholarly and Reference Division and
Palgrave Publishers Ltd (formerly Macmillan Press Ltd).

ISBN 0–333–73261–8

This book is printed on paper suitable for recycling and made from fully managed and sustained forest sources.

A catalogue record for this book is available from the British Library.

10   9   8   7   6   5   4   3
08   07   06   05   04   03   02   01

Printed in Malaysia

Contents

List of Tables and Figures

Tables

Figures

Preface

Since 1983, this book has had a considerable impact on the practice of many social workers. It contributed to our understanding of disability and, for me personally, it remained essential in my teaching. The strength of the book was that it did not attempt to provide simple answers to practising social work in a local authority, rather it required us to become actively involved in developing our practice from a new and more relevant theoretical base. As Mike Oliver said in its original introduction, a sub-title of this book might well have been 'The Social Model of Disability – A Paradigm for Social Work' and it was his hope that it would spawn a new and more exciting social work literature.

It is a matter of regret that, during the process of revision, I have found only a handful of people from within the social work profession who have taken on this challenge. Fortunately this was not true of disabled people and large numbers of individuals and groups from within the disabled people's movement have developed the social model of disability, drawing upon their experience, research and action. While their analysis is highly critical of the failure of social work to respond to the needs of disabled people, it is not without some hope that our profession still has the potential to do so. However, the need for change is urgent if social work is not to relegate itself as perpetually part of the problem.

To be asked to revise this book in 1997 was both a privilege and a pleasure. It has been a unique experience from which I have gained a lot. While many changes have taken place in the past 15 years which needed to be included within the text, it surprised me how much of the original remained valid even today. While this is obviously a complement to the writer, it also reinforces the criticisms of social work, which as a profession has failed to respond sufficiently to the challenge of the social model of disability.

Whilst writing is a single-minded task, it also requires support. I would like to thank three colleagues, Jennifer Harris,

Annie Huntington and Laura Middleton, for their help and comments at various stages. I also wish to thank Liz for her patience and understanding while I have excluded myself to the computer screen for nine months. Most of all I wish to thank Mike Oliver for asking me to do this and for his selfless support and comments throughout the writing. I have been given a very free rein to make the changes I felt were necessary so if any readers are disappointed by the result, I take responsibility.

Finally, I hope that this book is received as a positive contribution to changing the relationship between disabled people, social workers and the welfare state. It is intended as a vehicle for changing social work practice so, although I hope it will stand the test of time as well as the first edition, I also hope that it will contribute to itself becoming out of date.

University of Central Lancashire   BOB SAPEY

Introduction: Setting the Scene

Historically, social work could be said to have started with the formation of the Charity Organisation Society in the 1860s and it is just over a hundred years ago that the first hospital almoner was appointed. By the time of the Second World War, social work had become a reserved occupation but despite its development towards a profession – the gaining of university status for its training, its proactive stance in terms of child and health care and the influence of psychoanalysis on its practice – social work remained essentially concerned with administrating welfare on utilitarian principles.

The state was concerned to ensure that welfare be distributed on the basis that it would act as a remedy to dependency rather than as a sedative. The role of the early social workers was to assess the behaviour and motivations of individuals in need to determine how best to help them become self-reliant. The welfare policies of the postwar period introduced the concept of universalism as a means of removing the stigma attached to this distinction between the deserving and undeserving poor and this caused social work to re-evaluate its role.

The debates took many forms – genericism versus specialism, community versus individual, material versus emotional concerns and an independent versus a state-sponsored profession. However, in recent times social work has been replaced to a great extent by care management, and social policy has moved back to utilitarian principles with programmes such as the 'welfare to work' initiative of the 1997 Labour government. We find ourselves still with the question of what should be the relationship between social workers and their clients and, indeed, what is social work.

The term 'social work' as used here refers to organised professional activity carried out on behalf of individuals or groups of clients. This activity is geared towards the provision of services on an individual, group or community basis. The adjective 'professional' implies that those who provide these services are certified as competent to do so and are financially rewarded for so doing. The provision of such services does not merely involve the matching of need with resources but will also require professionals to be involved in ascertaining what needs are and arguing for adequate resources to meet those needs. The context of such activity may be a social services department, a hospital, residential accommodation, a voluntary organisation or any other appropriate agency. The range of methods involved will include casework, groupwork and community work, and these may be applied in a variety of settings including the home, residential care, day care and sheltered accommodation.

This is obviously a very broad definition of social work and flies in the face of the current trend to restrict social work to the management of services. While there may be adequate and justifiable reasons for calls upon social work generally to narrow its base of activity, it is not appropriate in the field of disability, for it will be argued throughout this book that disability is not an individual problem. Rather, it is a social problem concerned with the effects of hostile physical and social environments upon impaired individuals, or even a societal one concerned with the way society treats this particular minority group. As such, the base for social work activity with disabled people needs to be broadened, not narrowed. As has been argued for some time:

> Many disabilities are the result of social conditions and amenable to social services intervention. Medical care treatment, for example, is not going to solve the low-income, social isolation, and architectural barriers that are major for the disabled. At issue is the conflict over bureaucratic supremacy between the medical and social service parts of government. The clash involves ideological and theoretical differences concerning the nature of the problem and the response. (Albrecht and Levy, 1981:23)

There is also the question of the relationship between theory and practice in social work. There is much disillusionment with 'ivory-tower academics' whose theorising is not based upon the realities of practice, and again there may well be some justification for this disillusion in social work generally. The idea of social work as a practical activity is of course politically appealing and has led to the promotion of rational models of strategic management by the Social Services Inspectorate (1991a, b) and the adoption of competence outcomes for training by CCETSW. In terms of disability this approach is not new. Hanvey (1981) and Bell and Klemz (1981) both epitomise this approach. Both see the matching of needs and services as nonproblematic: there are *x* number of disabling conditions brought about by *y* causes; there is a legal and statutory framework, disabled people have a number of needs and there are these services provided to meet them. Such approaches ignore a number of crucial problems: What is 'need'? Are the services that are provided appropriate? Certainly Bell and Klemz (1981) show little awareness of the ways in which the feelings and aspirations of people with disabilities have changed radically.

If only social work with people with disabilities were as simple as this practical approach implies – the matching of resources to needs within a legal and statutory framework. It will be argued here that the dominant view of disability as a personal tragedy or disaster is an inaccurate one and may lead to the provision of inappropriate resources. It will further be suggested that social work as organised professional activity has either ignored disabled people or intervened on the basis of the dominant view of disability as a personal disaster. Chapter 1 will argue this at greater length and suggest a more appropriate theory of disability which will be referred to as the social model of disability and draw out some of its implications for practice.

This is not to assert the predominance of theory over practice but rather to suggest that there is a symbiotic relationship between the two: that theory will inform practice and orientate the activities of practitioners whose very activities will feed back and modify theory. This view is very close to what Kuhn (1962), in discussing the history and development of the natural sciences, called a 'paradigm'. A sub-title of this book might well be 'The Social Model of Disability – A Paradigm for Social Work', as originally noted by Mike Oliver.

Chapter 2 will then consider various ways of conceptualising disability and some of the implications that follow from these different conceptualisations. It will be suggested that the implication stemming from the individual model of disability is to count numbers of disabled people, compile registers and so on, whereas the social model suggests that ways need to be developed of measuring the disabling effects of the physical and social environment instead. Chapter 3 will focus on the relationship between impairment and disability in the context of social work practice with individuals, arguing that it is the task of social workers to be primarily concerned with reducing or alleviating the consequences of disability and not the problems of impairment.

Chapter 4 will widen the discussion and consider these issues in relation to social work practice with families where there is a disabled member. Chapter 5 will consider the role and functioning of residential and day-care facilities and will suggest that these services further disable impaired individuals. Suggestions as to how social work can attempt to prevent this imposition of additional disability will also be discussed.

Chapter 6 will consider the legal framework within which services are provided for disabled people, including the rights that disabled people have to access such services. Chapter 7 will pull together some of the issues raised in connection with the relationship of theory to practice and consider the implications both for service provision and professional practice that the social model of disability raises. It will review the progress made since this book was first published and, finally, some consideration will be given to ways forward into the next millennium.

1

Social Work and Disability: Old and New Directions

Prior to 1970 help for disabled people and their families was really only available through the health service (medical social workers) or voluntary organisations such as the Invalid Children's Aid Association and the Spastics Society. A few local authority health departments set up professional social work services in the 1950s, staffed mainly by medical social workers and in some cases occupational therapists as well. Welfare departments in the pre-Seebohm days also offered services to disabled people, but as most did not employ trained social workers little was done beyond material help and information-giving, while some provision was made for residential care. However, the Seebohm Report, local government reorganisation and the Chronically Sick and Disabled Persons Act 1970 was supposed to change all that and usher in a new era. Following this a number of other developments and reorganisations of social welfare, in particular the community care 'reforms' of the 1990s through the National Health Service and Community Care Act 1990 but also the Disabled Persons (Services, Consultation and Representation) Act 1986, the Children Act 1989 and the more recent Community Care (Direct Payments) Act 1996 have transformed the organisation of the statutory social services. Just what this has meant as far as social work with disabled people is concerned will thus be a major theme of this book.

The role of social services departments

In considering the development of services for physically disabled people the Seebohm Report will be taken as the starting-
point. While some, notably Brewer and Lait (1980), would
argue that this is the wrong place to start, the framework
proposed by Seebohm does highlight a number of areas of
concern that can be usefully considered. It also continues to
represent one of the more comprehensive sets of recommendations concerning social work with disabled people.
The Seebohm Report recommended the development of
services for disabled people in seven directions as follows:

1. Services for the physically handicapped are in urgent need
   of development.
2. A reasonably accurate definition of the size and nature
   of the multiple and complex problems of physical disability will require extensive research.
3. The social service department should be responsible for social
   work with physically handicapped people and their families,
   the provision of occupational therapy, residential and day
   centres for them, holidays, home helps, meals on wheels,
   sitters-in service, help with adaptations to houses and flats.
4. Substantial development is particularly required in the
   services for handicapped school leavers, and more thought
   and experiment is required to determine the best timing
   and methods of giving guidance on careers to physically
   handicapped children and young people.
5. Co-ordination of services for physically handicapped people
   requires a major effort in teamwork. It is impracticable
   at present to specify a particular form of organisation
   designed to achieve this everywhere.
6. The emphasis from the point of view of the social service department must be on helping the handicapped
   individual in the context of his family and community,
   and for this purpose a broadly based training and approach will be required.
7. It will be quite impossible for local authorities to run
   effective services for physically handicapped people without
   help from voluntary bodies.

(Seebohm Report, DHSS, 1968)

Based on Seebohm, the Local Authority Social Services Act 1970 established social services departments in their present form, and its recommendations on disability were incorporated into an additional Act, the Chronically Sick and Disabled Persons Act 1970. Unfortunately not only was this Act passed at a time of organisational upheaval when there were also the competing demands of other client groups, notably children, who had also been the beneficiaries of recent legislation, it also suffered from being inadequately resourced through the ambiguity of the money-order resolution that accompanied it as a private member's Bill (Topliss and Gould, 1981). The consequence of this has been that while the expectations of disabled people were raised, the new generic departments were unable to provide adequate support services either in terms of practical aid or emotional support (see Topliss and Gould, 1981; Knight and Warren, 1978; Shearer, 1981b).

By the mid-1980s social services were under pressure from two directions – first from disabled people who were dissatisfied with the lack of autonomy they could achieve through the process of provision of personal care services (Shearer, 1984) and its inequitable distribution (Feidler, 1988), and second from the government which was concerned with the spiralling costs of welfare services to adults (Audit Commission, 1986). The first of these resulted in the tabling of Tom Clarke's Disabled Persons (Services, Consultation and Representation) Bill and its attempt to ensure a voice for disabled people in the assessment of their needs. While succeeding at the parliamentary stage, the provisions of this Act were quickly superseded by the government's own proposals in 'Caring for People' (Department of Health, 1989) which sought to control expenditure through the introduction of a quasi-market into the social welfare sector. While this reinforced the role of local authorities as the arbiters of need, the disability movement continued to argue its case for greater control by disabled people of their own personal assistance (Oliver and Zarb, 1992; Morris, 1993; Zarb and Nadash, 1994). One of the results of these studies and the case they argued was the Conservative government's Community Care (Direct Payments) Act 1996 which amends the 1990 Act and fundamentally amends the National Assistance Act 1948, allowing money to be given to clients.

If consideration is given to each of the Seebohm recommendations separately, it is possible to make some reasonable estimate of progress in the last few decades. Certainly in
terms of recommendation 1, services initially developed though
it was clear that they still had a long way to go. As one study
has noted:

> Despite the substantial development of services for handi-
> capped people and the considerable increase of expendi-
> ture on these services . . . there were widespread indications . . .
> that even the most active departments could develop their
> services further. (Knight and Warren, 1978:70)

Ten years later Feidler (1988) described the provision of social
and housing services as a 'lottery' in that it would depend on
which authority area a disabled person lived in as to whether
they would receive the support needed to live independently.
Although some authorities may have made much progress,
this is certainly not the case everywhere.

Recommendation 2 suggested that a reasonably accurate
picture of the size and nature of the problem should be as-
certained, and this was built into the Chronically Sick and
Disabled Persons Act as a legal requirement. While all local
authorities have conducted their own surveys, the question of
accuracy remains. Most of these surveys only located approximately 50 per cent of the people that the government's own
survey (Harris, 1971) suggested there might be. This rapidly
changing picture continued with the second government survey (Martin *et al.*, 1988) from which the numbers of disabled
people using wheelchairs has been estimated at 360 000, while
less than 10 years later a survey of Disablement Services Centres found that this figure had risen to 710 000 (Aldersea,
1996). Clearly many of the surveys are now out of date and
this obviously affects their accuracy. Warren *et al.* (1979), in
following up their original survey in Canterbury, found that
13.4 per cent of the cohort had died, 4.9 per cent had left
the district and 5.1 per cent were in hospital or residential
care on a permanent basis. In addition they found considerable changes in the needs of people in their cohort, some
needing more help and others needing less. And of course

this study did not consider people who had become disabled in the meantime. It is obvious, therefore, that it is an extremely complex and time-consuming business maintaining an accurate picture of the needs of disabled people in a particular area. Indeed some have questioned the allocation of resources in this way, arguing it would be more productive to spend money on direct services rather than counting heads or updating registers.

With recommendation 3 the Seebohm Committee placed the onus on social services departments to provide a wide range of services, foremost among these being a social work service for disabled people and their families. Few, if any, departments would claim to provide such a service, and since the community care changes of 1993 the focus has moved away from social work. Other services such as residential and day care are often criticised, not on grounds of the failure to provide but rather in terms of what is actually provided – often 'segregated warehouses'. Durrant suggests that this is a defensive approach and that 'the large gymnasia-like buildings masquerading as day centres, and the purpose-built hostels which advertise the differentness from the rest of the street, typify this approach' (in Brechin *et al.*, 1981). Yet other services such as occupational therapy, holidays, meals-on-wheels, aids and adaptations are usually criticised on the grounds of the failure of departments to allocate adequate resources to them and not in terms of the kinds of services they provide.

Recommendation 4 suggested the development of services for disabled school-leavers. Following the recommendations of the 1978 Warnock Report, this has been left to the careers service, with each education authority in England and Wales employing specialist careers officers for disabled people. According to Rowan:

In July 1978, 6 per cent of young people under 18 registered as unemployed had been out of work for over 26 weeks, and $2\frac{1}{2}$ per cent for over a year; the equivalent figures for registered disabled young people were 30 per cent and 13 per cent. (Rowan, 1980:71)

By 1982 the situation was worsening with 23 per cent of unemployed non-disabled people under 25 years being out of work for more than 12 months, while the figure for disabled people was 41 per cent (NACEDP cited in Tisdall, 1994). For many years most social services departments were reluctant to attempt to identify the non-vocational needs of disabled young people for fear of the expectations and increased demands that might be created. This led to the passing of Sections 5 and 6 of the Disabled Persons (Services, Consultation and Representation) Act in 1986 which introduced formal procedures by which social services departments were obliged to communicate with education departments in order to identify and assess the social needs of disabled school leavers. While the actual provision of services remains the subject of rationing as for other social service clients, it has led to a much greater acceptance on the part of local authorities of their responsibilities, albeit with a high level of formalisation.

Improved coordination between services was identified as the fifth Seebohm recommendation. This remains a major problem, as Blaxter (1980) clearly identified and Phelan in his review of Seebohm unequivocally states:

> Effective co-ordination is as elusive as perpetual motion and if truly achieved verges on acquiring that very characteristic but frequently social provisions are either organised without acknowledgement of it or administered within a scope which endeavours to eliminate the need for it. *In services for people with handicaps, where generally co-ordination is required more than anywhere else paradoxically it is to be found the least.* (in Cypher, 1979:56, our emphasis)

The NHS and Community Care Act 1990 made inter-agency coordination mandatory and the emphasis from the Department of Health changed to one of cooperation. A range of guidelines and circulars were issued advising and instructing social services, health and housing authorities on how to ensure they worked together effectively. Critics would argue, however, that far from breaking down the barriers to cooperation and coordination, the introduction of market principles has created more impermeable boundaries determined by budgetary priorities and responsibilities.

The issue of training, which forms the basis of recommendation 6, was taken up by a Working Party convened by the Central Council for Education and Training in Social Work, whose major finding was encapsulated in its title (CCETSW, 1974): *People with Handicaps need Better Trained Workers*. Their major recommendations were for improved training at in-service, basic and post-qualifying levels. The introduction of the special option on 'handicap' as part of CSS courses and the considerable number of professionals from social services departments who have taken the Open University Course 'The Handicapped Person in the Community' improved matters a little, but both of these have been superseded by other developments. Following the introduction of the Diploma in Social Work (DipSW) in 1989 and the ending of the CSS and CQSW programmes, CCETSW encouraged social work departments in universities to develop disability options and to recruit disabled students (Stevens, 1991). By 1995, under increasing criticism from the government for its stance on anti-racist practice, CCETSW revised the DipSW towards a competence-based training, and while it is still possible to include disability within the curriculum it is argued (Froggett and Sapey, 1997) that this can only amount to an instrumental approach.

The final Seebohm recommendation was for closer cooperation between the statutory and the voluntary sector. There have been few, if any, studies of this relationship at local level, though voluntary sector provision extends from residential and day-care services to providing individual volunteers for gardening, driving people to appointments, and so on. Hatch, in his study of voluntary organisations in three towns, found:

At the local level most of the organisations for the handicapped worked quite closely with the statutory services. Where they did not do so it seemed in the three towns more a result of statutory neglect than antagonism on the part of the voluntary organisation. Within this kind of relationship the voluntary organisations were able to communicate needs, but seldom did they openly challenge the adequacy of existing provision by taking up an active pressure-group role. (Hatch, 1980:105)

Cooperation continues in this way with voluntary organisations and to some extent has been formalised through contracts with the statutory sector in their purchasing role. What has developed in relation to pressure groups has been the organisations 'of' disabled people. These groups of disabled people have consistently argued for a redefinition of the meaning of independence based on autonomy and control and have challenged the hegemonic structures within which welfare has been provided (see Campbell and Oliver 1996 for a full account of their development). They have not to any great extent taken over a provider role from the voluntary sector, and therefore have not entered into contracts with local authorities, but have achieved a notable success in campaigning for and demonstrating the advantages of direct payments.

Any attempts to assess accurately progress since Seebohm are obviously difficult, but in the light of what has been said it is not unreasonable to conclude that some progress has been made but there is still a long way to go. It is in the area of social work services specifically that least progress has been made, and in the rest of this chapter some of the reasons why this should be so will be considered before going on to outline some of the ways in which social work intervention with disabled people can be made more positive.

Social work services for disabled people

Specifically with regard to social work services, the CCETSW Working Party concluded that professionally trained social workers should be used:

(a) to provided personal social work help to the handicapped and their families on an individual, group or residential basis where, in addition to or arising from handicapping conditions, clients experience difficulties of a special nature (e.g. additional internal or external or environmental stress).

(b) to assess, with or without members of relevant other professions, the overall situation and specific needs.

(c) to provide, with or without the assistance of the remedial professions and vocational guidance staff, care, support, advice and guidance; and to assist whenever possible
in the process of rehabilitating those with handicaps.

(d) to advise, supervise and contribute to the training of
social service staff on the social work aspects of services
for those with handicaps and whenever possible to involve the clients in the process.

(e) to plan and co-ordinate services either alone or with
members of other disciplines, initiating plans based on
where the client is living, include the domiciliary supportive services and take into account all relevant community aspects.

(CCETSW, 1974)

While this sounds fine in theory, in practice social workers
(and especially qualified ones) have had a much more limited
role.

There have been a number of studies which have discussed
social work in relation to disabled people – few have been
complementary to social work. For example, Parsloe and
Stevenson (1978) found that the level and extent of social
work intervention with disabled people is relatively low. Occupational therapists or social work assistants in the main
provide most input to disabled people and their families.
Goldberg and Warburton (1979) found that social work intervention both lacked depth and fared badly in comparison with
work with other client groups. Their study showed that 30
per cent of cases dealt with by the intake team and 47 per
cent of long-term cases were problems involving physical disability. Of the total of 659 cases altogether, 80 per cent were
confined to agency review with the remainder only being allocated to individual social workers. In contrast, while cases
with child-care, delinquency and family problems produced
29 per cent of the intake cases and only 22 per cent of the
long-term ones, almost all of them were allocated to social
workers. At the time the Barclay Committee reported, these
and other studies confirmed that disabled people had less access
to skilled social work support, for as they noted:

Studies comparing caseloads of social workers of differing seniority tend to indicate that senior social workers and qualified social workers carry proportionately more cases of children in care, families with multiple problems or people with mental handicap or illness, whereas unqualified, inexperienced or assistant social workers carry proportionately more cases of physically handicapped and elderly people. (Barclay Committee, 1982:11)

Not only that, but social workers also failed to recognise the potential of working with disabled people, for, as Goldberg and Warburton (1979:93) asked: 'What aims did social workers pursue? In just under three-quarters of all the cases that were to remain open the preservation of the status quo was all the social workers hoped for'.

Another study found that social work intervention was even positively harmful, for, as Phillips and Glendinning found in a welfare rights project:

it was clear during the course of the project that information about other benefits had not been sent in any systematic way to the disabled people involved, and that although they were all known to their Social Services Department they had not received advice and encouragement to apply for benefits to which they were entitled. Indeed some people had even been given inaccurate information from social workers which had deterred them from making applications for benefits and caused subsequent financial losses. (Phillips and Glendinning, 1981:43)

Burgess (1982) writes of a case where, despite regular social work intervention, the disabled client has lost more than £4000 in unclaimed benefit in the previous few years.

In the late 1970s the Social Policy Research Unit at the University of York undertook an action research project whereby specialist social work support was provided for just over a hundred families with a disabled child, and the results of this specialist intervention were reinforced and compared with an equivalent number of families who did not have such support. The results, as the researchers concede (Glendinning,

1981), were 'both confusing and disappointing'. Certainly almost all of the families appreciated the personal support given by the specialist worker and agreed that it had made a substantial difference to them. However, there was little or no difference between the two groups on all other outcome measures such as the provision of aids, the take-up of benefits, and so on. These results can be interpreted in a number of different ways but do little to contradict the argument that social work support to disabled people and their families was in general inadequate.

While undoubtedly many social services departments and voluntary sector agencies established better services for disabled people during the 1980s, these are struggling to survive in the 1990s. The development of advisory (d'Aboville, 1991) or advocacy (Middleton, 1992) services that have been positively regarded by disabled people and their families are themselves under threat from the restricted understanding of outcome-based evaluation that has been popularised in the new public sector management. A particular result of the managerialisation of welfare during the 1980s and 1990s has been the conversion of many social work managers to the creed of quality assurance. This doctrine claims that it is of no importance who delivers or arranges a service so long as it is provided, but it contradicts much of the evidence from consumers of welfare (Howe, 1987; Morris, 1993; Willis, 1995) that the way in which social workers undertake their duties is important. It also ignores the wisdom of experience of the Poor Laws, that it was necessary for the administrators of welfare to 'humanise the relationship between the poor and authority – a difficult and complex task, and one which cannot be done by passing legislation' (Albert Evans MP quoted in Silburn, 1983) if they were to overcome the stigma attached to receiving assistance from the state. Social workers themselves and their organisations have been relatively powerless to challenge this shift from professionalism to managerialism because of their dependence on state sponsorship.

Furthermore the failure of social workers to develop an adequate theoretical and practice base for their interventions has led to criticisms, notably by disabled people themselves, who have accused social workers of ignorance about disabling conditions, benefits and rights, failing to recognise the need for practical assistance as well as verbal advice and to involve disabled people in the training process. They have also expressed resentment at being treated on a less than equal basis in the professional/client relationship (Finkelstein, 1991). In addition, while disabled people have been critical of social workers, social workers have often been reluctant to throw themselves wholeheartedly into work with this particular group. Certainly there are a number of reasons for this, which may include the following. First, low priority is given to work with this group and hence there are restricted career prospects within the statutory social services for anyone wishing to specialise in this type of work. Second, there is a lack of understanding of the potential of working with this group, for, as one writer puts it:

> Many people believe that work in the field of physical disability must be depressing because they have a vision of custodial care and of crippled lives filled with sadness and lost dreams. In actuality, rehabilitation of the physically disabled is especially rewarding because of the potential that exists in human beings in the face of stress, a potential that has seriously been underestimated. (Trieschmann, 1980, p. xi)

Third, as has already been said, inappropriate teaching about disability on some training courses can mean that workers feel inadequate or incompetent when working with disabled clients. Finally, personal fears about impairment can mean that workers may be reluctant to get involved in what they perceive to be the personal and social consequences of adjusting to a human tragedy or disaster. But the major criticism is that social workers, like all other professionals, have largely operated with inappropriate models or theories of disability, and it is in a sense perhaps fortunate that social work intervention has been so limited. There have of course been several attempts to change this both from within and without the profession (see for example Oliver, 1983, 1991; Holdsworth, 1991; Stevens, 1991; Middleton, 1992, 1995; Morris, 1993, 1997a; Swain *et al.*, 1993; Thompson, 1993) but there is little evidence that employers of social workers have made significant changes in the environments in which they practise. As Holdsworth points out:

> The practice of empowerment social work can thus be seen to entail a radical shift in attitudes on the part of the social worker, and ultimately on the part of Social Services Departments and society as a whole, if continual conflict between individual social worker and employing agency is to be avoided. However, as societal and Social Services Department views are unlikely to change sufficiently rapidly, the individual social worker is likely to experience at least periodic conflict with her employing agency as she aligns herself with her client in an attempt to fulfil a jointly agreed-upon service need. (Holdsworth, 1991:10)

Before going on to consider an appropriate model of social work intervention it is necessary to discuss why the current model is inappropriate. For this purpose the inadequate model will be referred to as the 'individual model' of disability, and this can be taken to include the medical model.

The individual model of disability

The individual model sees the problems that disabled people experience as being a direct consequence of their impairment. The major task of the professional is therefore to adjust the individual to the particular disabling condition. There are two aspects of this: first there is physical adjustment through rehabilitation programmes designed to return the individual to as near normal a state as possible; and, second there is psychological adjustment which helps the individual to come to terms with the physical limitations. It is not just that social work had accepted the dominant, individual model of disability which is deeply embedded in social consciousness generally, but also that the struggle for professional status and acceptance has been involved: 'In a search for professional status, social work has emphasised a medical, psychotherapeutic, individualised model of work because that seemed the best way of asserting its expertise and professionalism' (Wilding, 1982:97).

It is possible to be critical of both these aspects of adjustment, and it is the latter which will be focused upon as it is of most relevance to social work, though there have been criticisms of the former also (Brechin and Liddiard, 1981; Barnes, 1991). In order to criticise the psychological adjustment assumptions based on the individual model of disability, spinal-cord injury and blindness will be the impairments from which evidence will be drawn, though similar points can also be made about other conditions.

Starting from the assumption that something happens to the mind as well as to the body, a number of psychological mechanisms of adjustment have been identified, or more appropriately borrowed from other areas such as death and dying. Disabled individuals are assumed to have undergone a significant loss, and as a result depression may set in. In order to come to terms with this loss, a process of grieving or mourning will have to be worked through in a similar manner to those who must mourn or grieve for the loss of loved ones. Only when such processes have been worked through can individuals cope with death or disability.

Some writers have seen these mechanisms as a series of stages or steps which have to be worked through. A study by social workers (Weller and Miller, 1977) in New York University Hospital identified a four-stage process by which newly disabled paraplegics come to terms with their disability:

STAGE 1 SHOCK. The immediate reaction to the physical and psychic assault of spinal-cord injury often characterised by weeping, hysteria, and occasionally psychosis with hallucinations.

STAGE 2 DENIAL. A refusal to accept that complete recovery will not take place.

STAGE 3 ANGER. Often projected towards those physically active around them who serve as constant reminders of what has been lost.

STAGE 4 DEPRESSION. A realistic and most appropriate response to a condition of severe and permanent disability and a necessary stage if adjustment, rehabilitation and integration are to be achieved.

Thus the social work task is to help disabled individuals through these adjustment stages.

Albrecht (1976) characterises this and various other schemes as developmental models and argues that they all, at least partially, assume that:

1. an individual must move sequentially through all of these stages to become fully socialised;
2. there is but one path through the stages;
3. an individual can be placed clearly in one stage by operational criteria;
4. there is an acceptable time-frame for each stage and the entire process;
5. movement through the system is one way, that is, the system is recursive.

It is not just in the case of spinal-cord injury that such models are considered appropriate, for there are certainly similar ideas in the area, for example, of blindness. According to Carroll (1961:11), 'loss of sight is dying. When in the full current of sighted life blindness comes on a man, it is the end, the death, of that sighted life'.

In order to come to terms with this death, Fitzgerald (1970) identified four distinct phases in the typical reaction to the onset of blindness: disbelief, protest, depression and recovery. And indeed these become models for professional practice. For example, a young newly-blinded woman was told by a social worker in hospital that she could not have adjusted properly to her blindness as she was not depressed enough. Subsequent social work intervention was thus based on the need to work through this (non-existent) depression despite the fact that the woman involved was more concerned with problems about whether she would be able to continue in her job as a teacher, whether she would be able to continue to live alone and what aids she might need.

There are a number of general criticisms that can be levelled at individualistic theories or explanations. First, these theories implicitly picture the individual as determined by the things that happen to him or her – the adjustment to disability can only be achieved by experiencing a number of these psychological mechanisms or by working through a number of fixed stages. Second, adjustment is seen as largely an individual phenomenon, a problem for the disabled person, and as a consequence the family context and the wider social situation are neglected. Finally, such explanations fail to accord with the personal experiences of many disabled people who may not grieve or mourn or pass through a series of adjustment stages.

Further, it is not just those with spinal-cord injury who question such models. Clark, who lost his sight as a result of a war injury, states:

> The loss of sight need not and usually does not touch the core of a man's intellect and emotional being. What has changed is his relationship with the external world, a relationship with which he had grown so familiar that he scarcely thought of it.
>
> At this stage the very words we use about blindness become a little dubious. It is of course right to describe a war casualty as having been 'blinded', because the word conveys an idea of the violence of the event. There-after, however, he simply thinks of himself as lacking the visual sense images to which he had formerly been accustomed. It is something negative that has to be allowed for. He may at times refer to himself as being 'blind' so as to conform with verbal habits of the rest of the public. But privately he does not think of it in that way. Only when he falls into the pattern of ideas that others have of him, does he feel of himself as being 'in darkness'. (Clark, 1969:11–12)

Despite these criticisms, it would be true to say that these theories have made up the dominant, individual model of disability and this in itself needs to be explained. A major factor in this is that these theories are in accord with 'the psychological imagination' in that theorists who have imagined what it would be like to become disabled have assumed that it would be a tragedy and hence decided that such an occurrence would require difficult psychological mechanisms of adjustment. However, the psychological imagination may not be an appropriate starting-point for such theorising or research – it is surely a value judgement to assume that disability is a tragedy rather than that it is a phenomenon which may be explained in a number of ways. In the following chapter different meanings associated with disability will be discussed in more detail.

Another factor is that these explanations, being individualistic, are thereby politically convenient. When a disabled person fails to internalise the rehabilitation goals set by the professionals or persistently pesters his local social services department, he can be characterised as having problems in adjusting to his disability. This conveniently leaves the existing social world unchallenged; the goals of the rehabilitator remain unquestioned and the failure of the welfare department to provide the right assistance can be ignored.

While these and other factors may explain the adherence to these psychological theories, they do not explain why these theories have been empirically validated by a number of studies (Berger, 1988). In fact these theories may become self-fulfilling in at least two ways. At a methodological level, having conditioned research in the sense that they posit adjustment to disability as a problem, researchers then ask questions relevant to that problem and get answers which are then presented as findings, valid social facts. Prior to the criticisms of this model by disabled people there had been few, if any, studies which started out with the assumption that disability was not a problem. The following quote nicely illustrates the point:

Reflection on the many problems to which the cord injured person must make an adjustment impresses one with the gravity of the psychological processes which occur following cord injury.

Such an individual is confronted with grieving over his loss, coping with pain and phantom sensations, alterations in sexual functioning, loss of bladder and bowel control, the frustrations of immobilisation, loss of vocational goals and earning capacity, feelings of uselessness, role reversals in the family and the attendant loss of self-esteem and the social stigma of being 'different' in the public eye. *It is an amazing tribute to the flexibility and magnificence of the human spirit that so many people whose lives are thus devastated survive and function at the level of physical and social independence which most cord injured people achieve*. (Ibbotson, 1975:5, our emphasis)

This quote accurately reflects the process of 'sanctification' of disabled people which is deeply embedded in the social consciousness and reinforced through stereotyped media presentations. There is a polar opposite of this image which presents disability as a tragedy and personal disaster. As Shearer suggests:

> The 'norm' demands that people whose disabilities are obvious and severe must be at least 'sad' and even 'tragic'. And if that defence breaks down in the face of individual reality, it is ready with its own flip-side. The reaction of people who break out of the mould becomes: 'Aren't they wonderful?' (Shearer, 1981a:21)

In view of these images it is understandable that social workers are reluctant to get involved, for the scope of professional intervention with super-heroes or tragic victims must appear somewhat limited. However, the basic point remains: instead of questioning social reality with regard to disability, researchers simply proceed on the basis of taken-for-granted everyday meanings. But as so many paraplegics and blind people are able to function at a reasonable level, it is surely more logical to assume that this is a normal everyday reaction. To put the matter simply, adjustment may be normal and not a problem at all. And yet there had been few studies which started from the assumption of disability as normality prior to Shearer (1981a) and Finkelstein (1980).

There is a second way in which these theories may become self-fulfilling in that they may actually create the reality they purport to explain. In the case of mental illness it has been shown that psychiatrists impose their own definitions of the reality of particular problems upon their patients. Similarly in the study of criminal behaviour it has been shown that criminals will often verbalise theoretical explanations picked up in sessions with psychiatrists, psychologists and welfare workers as excuses for their behaviour even in compulsive crimes like pyromania, kleptomania and child molesting. With regard to disability, many disabled people will have contact with the theories described above, not through meeting academic psychologists or participating in research projects, but through the everyday contact with professional workers who are also internalising these theories. Professional journals have tended to disseminate these theories widely. An article in *Occupational Therapy* (Ibbotson, 1975) argued not only that individuals must experience the phases of shock, denial, turbulent aggression and working through, but also that there are a number of adaptations that patients must make, including adaptations in body-image, adaptation in role-image, loss of security and loss of self-esteem. A practising social worker expressed the following sentiments:

> Patients must be allowed to come to terms, they must grieve and mourn for their lost limbs, lost abilities or lost looks and be helped to adjust to their lost body-image. Personally, I doubt if anyone who has not experienced the onset of irreversible disability can fully understand the horror of the situation. (Dickinson, 1977:12)

Finkelstein, himself disabled, has argued that the use of such concepts is nothing less than the imposition of standards of able-bodied normalcy upon the meaning of disability for disabled individuals, partly engendered by the 'helper/helped' relationship:

> The attitude that a disabled person has 'suffered' a personal loss is a value judgment based upon an unspoken acceptance of the standard being able-bodied normalcy. But attributing loss to disabled people is not just the whim of certain helpers. The existence of helpers/helped builds into this relationship normative assumptions. 'If they had not lost something they would not need help' goes the logic 'and since it is us, the representatives of society doing the help, it is this society which sets the norms for the problem solutions'. (Finkelstein, 1980:17)

What is being suggested is that the psychological mechanisms and processes that research has identified and described are themselves the product of that research activity both as a result of its methodological predispositions and the spread of this knowledge to professionals who are then able to impose this definition of reality upon their clients. This is beautifully captured by Trieschmann, who asks:

> Is it possible that some of the publications that professionals have written reflect the requirement of mourning? Have professionals seen more stress and psychological difficulty than actually is present? Have professionals uncritically applied terms and theoretical concepts from the field of 'mental illness' to describe the 'normal reaction to an abnormal situation' which onset of spinal injury represents? Have professionals been describing phenomena that do not exist? Have professionals in clinical interactions placed disabled persons in a 'Catch 22' position? If you have a disability, you must have psychological problems: if you state you have no psychological problems, then this is denial and that is a psychological problem. And because this is so, have psychologists, psychiatrists, social workers and rehabilitation counsellors lost credibility with other rehabilitation personnel and with persons who have spinal cord injury, and rightly so? (Trieschmann, 1980:47)

And it is not just a matter of losing faith but, as she points out, disabled people 'have felt victimised by professionals who write articles about the reactions to spinal cord injury that are based more on theory than fact' (Trieschmann, 1980: xii).

The unquestioning use by social work of psychological and physiological explanations of disability has been reinforced during the 1990s, a period in which welfare has been technologised. The process of compartmentalising and coding 'abnormality' that is derived from the individual model and that drives the World Health Organisation's (1980) International Classification of Impairment, Disability and Handicap (ICIDH), becomes attractive and administratively convenient to welfare managers who are keen to account for what has always been the difficult to define practice of social work. The introduction of new technology with an algorithmic basis of analysis naturally leads to the selection of explanations that permit some quantifiable form of linking behaviour and need. Rather than seeking to understand the nature of the relationship between impairment and disability, the instrumentally-driven bureaucratic processes that prevail (Blaug, 1995) seek an analysis that is compatible with the technology, and therefore it is of little surprise that the use of such classification systems are promoted as the way forward for social welfare (Ypren, 1996).

Despite the long-standing criticisms, it is clear that the individual model remains the dominant one with regard to disability and it has perhaps taken on the attributes of what Kuhn (1962) has called a 'paradigm' – that is, a body of knowledge to which all those working in the field adhere. However, the same writer has shown that paradigms are sometimes replaced or overthrown by 'revolution', and this revolutionary process is often sparked by one or two criticisms of the existing paradigm. Only then can a new paradigm develop to replace the old. Having provided one such criticism, it is now worth considering what a new paradigm – a 'social model' of disability – might look like.

A social model of disability

This new paradigm involves nothing more or less fundamental than a switch away from focusing on the physical limitations of particular individuals to the way the physical and social environments impose limitations upon certain groups or categories of people. Shearer captures the need for this change in paradigm in her criticism of the International Year of Disabled People:

> The first official aim of the International Year of Disabled People in 1981 was 'helping disabled people in their physical and psychological adjustment to society'. The real question is a different one. How far is society willing to adjust its patterns and expectations to include its members who have disabilities, and to remove the handicaps that are now imposed on their inevitable limitations? (Shearer, 1981a:10)

Adjustment within the social model, then, is a problem for society, not for disabled individuals.

For some, however, it is not just a matter of society's willingness to adjust its patterns and expectations but one of removing the social oppression which stems from this failure to adjust. One statement of this comes from the Union of Physically Impaired Against Segregation (UPIAS), who state:

In our view, it is society which disables physically impaired people. Disability is something imposed on top of our impairments by the way we are unnecessarily isolated and excluded from full participation in society. To understand this it is necessary to grasp the distinction between the physical impairment and the social situation, called 'disability', of people with such impairment. Thus we define impairment as lacking part of or all of a limb, or having a defective limb, organism or mechanism of the body: and disability as the disadvantage or restriction of activity caused by a contemporary social organisation which takes no or little account of people who have physical impairments and thus excludes them in the mainstream of social activities. Physical disability is therefore a particular form of social oppression. (UPIAS, 1976:3–4)

While both Shearer and UPIAS are advocating a social model of disability, there are differences in their views which need to be acknowledged. Shearer is asking society (that is, able-bodied society) to remove the disabilities imposed upon impaired individuals, whereas UPIAS argue that such disabilities will only be removed by disabled people themselves engaged in active 'struggles'. Thus the former sees the reduction or removal of disability as something which may be given, whereas the latter see them as having to be fought for. There are obviously different implications for professional practice stemming from these views, which can be encapsulated in asking professionals whether they wish to work for disabled people or with them.

This social model of disability, like all paradigms, fundamentally affects society's world-view and, within that, the way particular problems are seen. If the problem of housing for disabled people is taken as an example, the individual model focuses on the problems that disabled people encounter in terms of getting in and out, bathing, access to the kitchen, the bedroom, and so on. In short the approach focuses on the functional limitations of individuals in attempting to use their own environment. The social model, however, sees disability as being created by the way housing is unsuited to the needs of particular individuals. Thus we have 'housing disability'. A housing research project in Rochdale (Finlay, 1978) attempted to operationalise this concept by taking as given the 'reduced performance capabilities' of particular individuals and measuring instead the restrictions that unsuitable housing environments place upon the individuals concerned. The implications of this approach for professionals involves a switch in emphasis away from the provision of personal aids (most of which are not used in any case) and remedial therapy, and a move towards adapting environments so that they do not unduly restrict people with functional limitations.

The longer-term policy implications of this approach centre on:

> whether the policies most suited to their needs should adopt a preventative approach, in the form of more suitable housing provided in the community, or a remedial approach in the form of para-medical support provided either in the home or special institutions by people whose very intervention, if made unnecessarily, is by itself a disabling factor in the lives of physically handicapped people. (Finlay, 1978:15)

The same perspective can provide important insights in other areas: the well-known problems of finding out about benefit entitlements are examples of 'information disability' (Davis and Woodward, 1981). Davis and Woodward go on to argue that it is not just the physically impaired who suffer from information disability but

> for those such as people who are physically impaired, where access to specialist information is crucial to meaningful participating, there is a significant distinction. Information disability is a specific form of social oppression. In practice, it results in the disadvantage or restriction of activity caused not by the impairment of the individual – but by the way in

our society we present, or withhold, information and prevent opportunity for full participation in the mainstream of social life. (Davis and Woodward, 1981)

When applied to the world of work the social model of disability provides equally valuable insights:

The world of work (buildings, plant, machinery, processes and jobs, practices, rules, even social hierarchies) is geared to able-bodied people, with the objective of maximising profits. The growth of large-scale industry has isolated and excluded disabled people from the processes of production, in a society which is work centred. (Swain, 1981:11–12)

This is crucial in late capitalist society, where individuals are still judged upon what they do and appropriate social status thereby accorded. Hence it is not difficult to see that the dominant social perception of disabled people as 'dependent' stems not from their inability to work because of their physical limitations, but because of the way in which work is organised in modern industrial society.

According to Finkelstein (1980), this social model of disability may be most appropriately applied to physical impairments, but it can also take in sensory impairments. For example, deaf people may be disabled by the increasing use of the telephone which restricts people who can communicate perfectly adequately at a face-to-face level, or meetings may be held in badly lit rooms so that they cannot adequately see other participants and follow their lips. Harris (1995) suggests that deaf people who use British Sign Language (BSL) suffer disadvantages from linguistic isolation in employment situations where the majority of workers are hearing. In fact, pressure is exerted upon deaf workers to behave as much like hearing workers as possible – in effect to 'deny' and invisibilise their deafness. She argues that many deaf people work in situations where there is a complete lack of meaningful communication between themselves and colleagues. The disadvantages suffered by deaf people stem from a lack of tolerance and respect for linguistic difference by management and co-workers and as such, become individualised as a problem for deaf workers to solve, rather than for hearing people to view as a challenge (Harris, 1997). However, Harris suggests that such a change in attitudes by hearing people and a willingness to learn BSL could radically alter the pattern of disadvantage and provide an empowering environment for deaf people.

Similarly, learning difficulties can be seen as less the problem of the intellectual impairment of certain individuals but more related to general expectations about levels of social competence. As Dexter wrote:

> In our society, mental defect is even more likely to create a serious problem than it is in most societies because we make demonstration of formal skill at coordinating meanings (reading, writing and arithmetic) a requirement for initiation into adult social status, although such skills are not necessarily related to the capacity for effective survival or economic contribution. (in Boswell and Wingrove, 1974:294)

Since its development there have been criticisms of the social model. Morris (1991) raised the concern that the social model may be just as oppressive as the individual model if it is imposed in such a way as to deny the experience of individuals. Drawing on feminist criticisms of male theorising, she suggests that the danger lies in attempting to compatmentalise the personal feelings and experiences of people rather than grounding the political analysis in them. Crow (1996) supports this position and calls for the inclusion of impairment in the theorising of the social model:

> We need to take a fresh look at the social model of disability and learn to integrate all its complexities. It is critical that we recognise the ways in which disability and impairment work together. The social model has never suggested that disability represents the total explanation or that impairment doesn't count – that has simply been the impression we have given by keeping our experiences of impairment private and failing to incorporate them into our public political analysis. (Crow, 1996:66)

Some disabled people do experience the onset of impairment as a personal tragedy which, while not invalidating the argument that they are being excluded from a range of activities by a disabling environment, does mean it would be inappropriate to deny that impairment can be experienced in this way. However, while such reactions themselves may be due to the extent to which the norms and values attached to the individual model have embedded themselves within our psyche, the values of the social model have been shown to be effective in combatting them. Tate *et al.* (1992) reported on a study which showed that people with spinal injuries who were put on an 'independent living program' at the time of their acute rehabilitation, were able to adjust to their new circumstances with less negative psychological effects than those who received a more traditional, medically-orientated service. Individual disabled people have borne testament to the value of the social model to them personally:

> My life has two phases: before the social model of disability, and after it. Discovering this way of thinking about my experiences was the proverbial raft in stormy seas. It gave me an understanding of my life, shared with thousands, even millions, of other people around the world, and I clung to it. (Crow, 1996:56)

Some researchers have attempted to incorporate a model of impairment that is consistent with the social model of disability. Creek *et al.* (1987) in their study of the social implications of spinal injury, used the theoretical approach of viewing impairment as a significant life event. As with other life events, individual reactions are related to a range of social and personal factors. This interactionist approach takes into consideration the prior experience of individuals and acknowledges the impact this will have on the adjustment they make to change, while also being consistent with the social model of disability.

A different criticism of the social model has been raised by Stuart (1994) who suggests that the social model has tended to be an exclusive analysis that has failed to acknowledge the multiple oppression of black disabled people. He explains:

The oppression of medicalisation and the potential for empowerment of the social model is as relevant to black disabled people as it is to any other disabled people. The legitimate point of view of this group should be perceived as, perhaps, broadening our understanding of the disabling process and the methods of achieving empowerment. It should also be acknowledged that these people might not accept that the social model, as it is currently theorised, will provide the intended liberation. To do so, it is important to acknowledge that disability itself has been racialised. In other words, the perception of disability differs depending upon the colour of an individual's skin or his or her ethnic identity. (Stuart, 1995:372)

The experience of black disabled people suggests that racism is operating within the disability movement just as it is operating within other institutions in Britain and that organisations of disabled people are not in some way exempt or immune from acting oppressively towards black people. Given the ways in which black disabled people experience the provision of social work services as racist (Begum *et al*., 1994), it is clearly necessary for the social model of disability to incorporate an understanding of these differing perceptions of disability if it is to provide an analysis that is inclusive.

The overriding importance of this social model of disability is that it no longer sees disabled people as having something wrong with them – it rejects the individual pathology model. Hence when disabled people are no longer able to perform certain tasks, the reasons are seen as poor design of buildings, unrealistic expectations of others, the organisation of production or an unsuitable housing environment. This inability does not stem, therefore, from deficiencies in the disabled individual. As Finkelstein (1980:25) points out, 'The shift in focus from the disabled person to the environment implies a shift in the practical orientation of workers in the field.' What does this mean for social work? It is this question which will now be briefly considered.

The social model and its implications for social work

The social work profession has failed to give sustained consideration to physical disability either in terms of theory or practice, and evidence for this view can be found by comparing the number of books that have been written about the subject with, say, the number written about children. Prior to 1983 there were none solely devoted to the topic of social work and physical disability and since then only a handful, and while this is only one example of social work's lack of sustained interest, it is nevertheless a powerful one. This is certainly so when one considers that in recent years social workers have been very keen to write about a whole range of other topics from sex therapy to community work, from children and families to death and dying, from juvenile delinquents to mental health.

However, as was suggested earlier, it is perhaps fortunate that there has been this lack of interest, for social work has adopted the wrong model of disability. The outlining of a social model of disability in the last section before now going on to discuss some of its implications for social work practice goes against the current conventional wisdom which suggests that theory should be practice-based rather than the other way round. Nevertheless, to rely on practice to inform theory when practitioners may have already internalised an inappropriate model is to invite disaster, for it would merely result in reinforcement of the individual model of disability at a theoretical level. Therefore, an attempt has been made to lay the theoretical base before considering some of the practice implications. This discussion will inevitably be brief, as it is for practitioners themselves to work out, in conjunction with their disabled clients, the full implications, and not for academics to extract practice blueprints from their theories.

If consideration is given to the three main social work approaches (casework, groupwork and community work), it is possible to make a number of statements relevant to practice. For example, the switch from an individual to a social model of disability does not signify the death of casework. Rather, it sees casework as one of a range of options for skilled intervention. It does not deny that some people may grieve or mourn for their lost able body, but suggests that such a view should not dominate the social worker's assessment of what the problem may be. Blaxter cites one such example of

Mr Miller, a young family man with a progressive disabling disease, went to seek the advice of a social worker about his problems, which he was defining in entirely practical terms. In particular he wanted a confused social security position clarified. He returned a little bewildered: 'I don't really know what was going on. I just wanted these forms filled in. She kept on talking about the disease – what I felt about it what the wife felt about it. Coming to terms with it. All I want to come to terms with is these forms!' (Blaxter, 1980:123)

Thus grief work or bereavement counselling may be appropriate in some cases but not in all or even most. Some disabled people, particularly those suffering from progressive diseases, may need long-term support of the kind that only a casework relationship can provide, and building upon the idea of the disabled family, the whole family may indeed become the target for casework intervention (see Lenny, 1993 and Oliver, J. 1995 for discussion of counselling and the social model of disability).

Similarly, groupwork need not focus solely on the need to create a therapeutic environment in which individuals or families can come to terms with disability. Groups can also be used to pool information on particular benefits, knowledge on where and how to get particular services, and even on a self-help basis to give individuals the confidence to assert that their disability does not stem from their physical impairments but from the way society often excludes them from everyday life. In addition, the group can be used as the major means of giving disabled people back responsibility for their own lives, as is described in a discussion on residential care:

meetings in the small residential groups were a forum for staff and residents to plan their activities and to determine priorities. They gave the opportunity for residents to take responsibility for themselves and also for the staff to do 'social work'. (Dartington *et al.*, 1981:52–3)

The potential for intervention using community work methods is also exciting. There have already been a number of local access groups which focus on the way the physical environment disables people, and numerous access reports and guides have been produced. A few community workers have organised 'forum' meetings of all organisations of and for disabled people in a particular locality and these have proved useful in confronting local authorities about cut-backs, in ensuring that the needs of disabled people are taken into account in pedestrianisation schemes, and so on. And if the definition of 'community' is expanded beyond its strictly geographical meaning to take in the idea of moral communities (Abrams, 1978) or psychic communities (Inkeles, 1964) or what the Barclay Committee (1982) referred to as 'communities of interest', then it is possible to see community work methods being used in disability organisations. For example the Spinal Injuries Association employs a welfare officer whose job is one of enabling its members to work out their own problems and solutions by utilising the collective wisdom and experiences of its 3000 paraplegic members through mutual support, peer counselling and the provision of information and advice (see d'Aboville, 1991).

In suggesting that theory should inform practice with regard to physical disability rather than vice versa, a number of developments in social work practice compatible with the social model of disability have obviously been ignored. There have undoubtedly been initiatives by individual social workers or departments which are not based on the individual model and which are indeed perfectly compatible with a social model of disability, but social work as a profession has not given systematic attention to developing a theoretical perspective on disability. Even within the vastly growing literature on anti-discriminatory practice there is little evidence of a sustained application of the combatting of oppression in relation to disability. Rather it is notable that the construction of dependency is largely missing from the analysis of women as carers, and that the dominance of the individual model prevents social workers from making links between the analysis of racism in social work and disablism.

Such theory has been developed elsewhere, notably by disabled people and their organisations. As a consequence theory and practice have proceeded separately and have not merged into what was earlier called a 'paradigm' in respect of the individual model. It is crucial, however, that in future there is a merger between theory and practice in order to create an alternative paradigm to the one based on the individual model. Only then will the social model replace the individual one, which has proved so ineffective in meeting the needs of disabled people and so unattractive to professionals working in the field.

Conclusions

To conclude this critical overview, it has been suggested that the track record of social work involvement with disabled clients has not been good. Social workers have either ignored disabled people and their needs, or when they have been involved their interventions have been based on inappropriate assumptions about the nature of disability. Certainly social work has failed to develop its theory and practice in terms of even the Seebohm view of seeing the disabled person in the context of family and community, let alone taking on board the implications of a fully developed social model of disability. There are of course reasons for this. Social work, like all other professions, has been unable to shake loose from the individual model embedded in social consciousness generally. It is also of course politically convenient to have the problem located in the individual – repeated requests for assistance can be explained away as signs of having a 'chip on the shoulder' or of a 'failure to adjust to disability'. More recently the institutional structures within which social work operates have been organised to focus on the provision of services within strict budgetary limits. The rhetoric of 'needs-led' services have been outweighed by the instinct of organisations to ensure they are above criticism from a judicial review of their activities that would interpret need from an individual model.

The social model of disability has been articulated not just by individual disabled people but increasingly by a number of disability organisations. For, as Finkelstein suggests:

Disabled spokesmen and spokeswomen have become increasingly active in articulating their own perceptions of their situation. Since the Second World War there has been a rapid growth in the numbers and size of organisations of disabled people and increasingly, particularly during the past decade, a growing group identity. (Finkelstein, 1980:1)

At the time it was possible to identify three distinct approaches adopted by these groups: the incomes approach, the self-help approach, and the populist approach. All of these approaches, to a greater or lesser extent, built upon the social model of disability, and such activities have tended to become consolidated, further exposing the contradictions between the individual and social models of disability.

The social work profession has made some attempts to join with disabled people and their organisations, for example the BCODP–BASW conference in Birmingham in 1986. It is ideally placed to play a crucial part in the development of a new paradigm as it is less tied to the individual model of disability than the medical and paramedical professions, and it has a range of methods of work, skills and techniques which are well-suited to working within the social model of disability. The rewards for social workers will arise from the enhanced professional and personal satisfaction that will stem from both the increased range of tasks in which to exercise professional skills and the greater potential for achieving change. In working with disabled people the social work task is no longer one of adjusting individuals to personal disasters, but rather helping them to locate the personal, social, economic and community resources to enable them to live life to the full.

In the following chapters some of the themes developed here will be pursued in relation to issues concerning social work practice. It should be re-emphasised, however, that this does not mean that what follows will be a practical manual on 'how to do social work with disabled people within the social model of disability'. Rather, it will be an orientating perspective enabling social workers to develop their practice in conjunction and partnership with their disabled clients.

2

Thinking about Disability

A major theme of this book is that social work, as an organised professional activity, has given little thought to the problems of disability, and where it has it has merely reproduced
traditional thinking in its application to social work practice.
A second theme is that much of this traditional thinking about
disability is inaccurate and incorrect at least in that it is in-
congruent with the personal experiences of many disabled
people. A third theme will be to develop more appropriate
thinking about disability and to draw out some of its implications for the practice of social work.

There are three main sources upon which to draw when
considering the question 'What is disability?' There is social
consciousness generally, there are professional definitions of
disability and there are personal realities, as articulated by
disabled people themselves. Each of these sources needs to
be considered separately.

General views of disability

medical?

It has already been suggested that the now dominant view of
disability is one of personal tragedy or disaster. However, this
is not true of all societies, and some may regard disability as
a sign of being chosen, of possession by God or the devil. In
short, disability does not have meanings which are similar in
all cultures, nor indeed within the same culture is there always agreement about what disability actually is. As two anthropologists have noted:

> A class of persons grouped together under the term 'physi-
> cally handicapped' is at best difficult to treat as ethnological

data. Here for us is a category of persons with social liabilities peculiar to the conditions of our society. It represents no logical or medical class of symptoms. For example, carrot-colored hair is a physical feature and a handicap in certain social situations, but a person with this characteristic is not included in this class. Nor is the symptom itself the only criterion, for though the person afflicted with infantile paralysis may limp as a result of the disease and be deemed to be handicapped, yet the person with an ill-fitting shoe or a boil on his foot who also limps will be excluded.

When one introduces the concepts of other cultures than our own, confusion is multiplied. Even assuming the existence of such a class in other societies, its content varies. The disfiguring scar in Dallas becomes an honorific mark in Dahomey. (Hanks and Hanks, 1980:11)

Variations in cultural views of disability are not just a random matter, however, but differences may occur as a result of a number of factors, some of which have been identified by the same two anthropologists:

The type of economy is a factor with its varying production units, need for manpower, amount of surplus and its mode of distribution. The social structure is important, whether egalitarian or hierarchical, how it defines achievement, how it values age and sex. (Hanks and Hanks, 1980:13)

The type of economy is obviously an important factor in this variation: restricted mobility is less likely to be a problem in an agricultural society than in a hunting and gathering one. And, as has already been suggested, the way production is organised also has implications for 'the speed of factory work, the enforced discipline, the time-keeping and production norms – all these were a highly unfavourable change from the slower, more self-determined and flexible methods of work into which many handicapped people had been integrated' (Ryan and Thomas, 1980:101).

The social structure and values of a society are also important in shaping cultural views of disability. A hierarchical structure like Britain's, based upon values of individual success through personal achievement, inevitably means that most disabled people will be low in the hierarchy on the basis of their reduced ability to compete on equal terms with everyone else. Societies whose central values are religious may well interpret disability as punishment for sin or possession by the devil, or as a sign of being chosen by God. These and other factors shape social attitudes to disability. The point is that the general view of disability as a personal disaster, an individual tragedy, is culturally specific to Britain and not necessarily the only view. Certainly the view of disability as a personal disaster is a common one in modern industrial societies but there are considerable variations in professional conceptions of disability and their implications for the provision of services and for professional intervention. Scott (see Douglas, 1970) has clearly demonstrated this in his analysis of blindness in the USA, Sweden, Britain, Italy and France. The rest of this chapter is concerned with the way this general view is translated into professional conceptions of disability in Britain and the implications of this for social work.

Current professional definitions of disability

Brechin and Liddiard (1981) have suggested that there may be as many as 23 different professionals involved with a disabled individual, though they do not, of course, all use different definitions. Townsend (1979) has suggested that these definitions can be divided into five broad categories: abnormality or loss, clinical condition, functional limitation, deviance and disadvantage. No single one of these is right or wrong, but rather they are developed for specific purposes or situations, and all can be criticised on various grounds.

1. *Abnormality or loss*. This may be anatomical, physical or psychological loss, it may refer to loss of a limb or part of the nervous system or of a sense modality (for example deafness or blindness). The existence of either may not necessarily be disabling. Someone who has lost both legs may well have a very hectic social life, whereas someone else

with a minor facial blemish may never go out because of it.
2. *Clinical condition.* This will refer to diseases or illnesses which
   alter or interrupt physical or psychological processes. Arthritis, epilepsy, bronchitis and schizophrenia are examples
   of such definitions. Diagnosis, however, is often difficult
   with conditions like schizophrenia or epilepsy, and the
   government has been involved in controversies over whether
   a number of ex-miners have bronchitis or pneumoconiosis.
   If they have the former, they are not entitled to compensation; whereas if they have the latter, they are. Learning
   difficulties is another difficult area, for there is often no
   clinical diagnosis but rather attempts to assess social competence, or possibly measure IQ.
3. *Functional limitations of everyday activities.* This refers to the
   inability, or at least restricted ability, to perform normal
   personal or social tasks such as washing and dressing, doing the shopping, negotiating steps or going to the cin-
   ema. There are obvious difficulties in establishing objective
   standards against which abilities can be measured and which
   take account of other factors such as age, sex and motiva-
   tion. External factors are also important: someone in a
   wheelchair in a non-adapted house may be limited func-
   tionally, but not in an adapted one. Additionally this definition often leads to the debatable assertion that 'we will
   all be disabled one day', in that everyone becomes func-
   tionally limited by the ageing process. This is normal and
   expected and while various professional definitions may
   regard many old people as disabled, it does not follow that
   they themselves, or society at large, agree with this definition.
4. *Disability as deviance.* There are two separate aspects of this
   that need to be considered: first, deviation from accepted
   physical and health norms; and second, deviation from behaviour appropriate to the social status of particular individuals or groups. In seeing disability as deviation from
   particular norms, the problem arises in specifying what those
   norms are and who defines them. A similar problem arises
   with regard to deviant behaviour: Who specifies what normal and appropriate behaviour are, and with reference to
   what? Deviation from behaviour appropriate to the able-
   bodied or behaviour appropriate to disabled normality?

5. *Disability as disadvantage.* This refers to the allocation of resources to people at specific points in the social hierarchy, and in the case of disabled people they often receive less than their able-bodied counterparts. This broadens the concept of disability considerably, for it is not just those with physical impairments who are socially handicapped – so are illiterates, alcoholics and one-parent families, plus, perhaps, ethnic minorities and women.

Thus there are a number of definitions of disability, none of which presents the whole picture or is the right answer, for, as Townsend puts it:

Although society may have been sufficiently influenced in the past to seek to adopt scientific measures of disability, so as to admit people to institutions, or regard them as eligible for social security or occupational or social services, these measures may now be applied in a distorted way, or may not be applied at all, or may even be replaced by more subjective criteria by hard-pressed administrators, doctors and others. At the least, there may be important variations between 'social' and objective assessments of severity of handicap. (Townsend, 1979:688)

In the remainder of this chapter functional definitions will be considered in more detail, particularly in view of the fact that functional definitions are currently the ones upon which access to social services departments and the services they provide usually depend.

Functional definitions of disability

There have been various piecemeal attempts to gather statistics about disabled people, beginning with the census of 1851 which asked questions about blindness and deafness. However, these questions were dropped in 1921 and for 70 years no census attempted to gather information about disability, largely on the methodological grounds that it is too difficult to frame appropriate questions in such a general survey. The

1991 census included a question asking respondents if any member of their household had a 'limiting long-term illness' which may well equate to impairment for large numbers of people but is not necessarily reliable as a measure of disability. Legislative measures like the recently repealed Disabled Persons (Employment) Act 1944 and the National Assistance Act 1948 required that registers be kept, but only for those in receipt of services, not as any systematic attempt to estimate numbers and establish needs. By the 1960s it was obvious that there was little data available to facilitate the expansion of services for disabled people as part of the general programme of increased welfare expenditure. Accordingly, the then Ministry of Health instigated a research programme which was to culminate in the mammoth study by the Office of Population Censuses and Surveys (Harris, 1971; Buckle, 1971) whereby nearly a quarter of a million households were surveyed. The exercise was repeated with some methodological changes in 1986 (Martin *et al.*, 1988) when 100 000 private households and an unstated number of communal establishments were screened. From the first survey 8538 households were followed up and interviewed in-depth, while the second involved approximately 10 000 adults in private households and 4000 in communal establishments.

Functional assessments of disability were used in both these studies and although there was some change in the wording of the definitions they were both based on the World Health Organisation's definitions of impairment, disability and handicap as follows:

Impairment
'Any loss or abnormality of psychological, physiological or anatomical structure or function.' Here we are dealing with parts or systems of the body that do not work.

Disability
'Any restriction or lack (resulting from an impairment) of ability to perform an activity in the manner or within the range considered normal for a human being.' Here we are talking about things people cannot do.

Handicap

'A disadvantage for a given individual, resulting from an impairment or disability, that limits or prevents the fulfilment of a role (depending on age, sex and social and cultural factors) for that individual.' This is in relation to a particular environment and relationships with other people.

(Martin *et al.*, 1988:7)

The measurement of extent of 'handicap' in the first study was based on a series of questions regarding people's capacity to care for themselves. The response to each question was graded according to whether the activity could be managed without difficulty, with difficulty, or only with help. Some activities were regarded as more important than others and measurements were weighted accordingly. The most important items were:

1. getting to and using the toilet
2. eating and drinking
3. doing up buttons and zips

Other items were:

4. getting in and out of bed
5. having a bath or all-over wash
6. washing hands and face
7. putting on shoes and stockings
8. dressing other than shoes or socks
9. combing and brushing hair (women only)
10. shaving (men only)

The responses to these questions were collected, and as a consequence disabled people were divided into four categories: (i) very severely handicapped, (ii) severely handicapped, (iii) appreciably handicapped, and (iv) impaired. According to this functional measurement, it was estimated that there were 3 071 000 impaired people, or 7.8 per cent of the total population. In terms of the categories of handicap, Harris estimated the following numbers in each category:

Very severely handicapped	157 000
Severely handicapped	356 000
Appreciably handicapped	616 000
Impaired	1 942 000
	3 071 000

The Harris survey also highlighted two other important facts: that handicap increases with age; and that disabled women begin to outnumber disabled men in the older age groups as shown in Table 2.1.

Overall there were considerably more disabled women in the population than there were disabled men, but within the age structure there are significant variations. In fact up to the age of 50 both in sheer numbers and prevalence more men were likely to be defined as disabled than women. Two possible reasons are: (i) many more men work and risk disablement through accidents and work-induced illnesses, and (ii) many more young males partake in dangerous sports and leisure activities, for example motor-cycle riding, rugby, mountaineering, and so on. Consequently these figures reflect sexual divisions within society whereby certain activities, both work and leisure, are dominated by males. After the age of 50, then, not only are there more disabled women but their prevalence in the population is also greater. This is a reflection of the fact that women live longer than men, coupled with the fact that prevalence of a significant number of impairing conditions increases with ageing. Additionally, of course, functional definitions of disability use measures of physical capabilities, and as these inevitably decline with ageing more and more elderly people are defined as disabled.

The gender differences are more pronounced when looking at particular groups of disabled people. Sapey (1995), for example, found that there were twice as many women as men in receipt of NHS wheelchairs from one Disablement Services Centre (DSC) in 1993, a pattern we have confirmed by repeating the exercise with a different DSC in 1996. While the bulk of this difference was made up of people over 65 years of age, it began to appear in the 35 to 40 age group. Below this age there is a slightly higher incidence of wheelchair use amongst men. It should be noted, however, that Aldersea (1996)

Table 2.1 *Prevalence per 1000 (and estimated numbers in '000s in brackets) of men and women in different age groups, in private households in Great Britain, with some impairment – 1971*

Age group	Men		Women		Men and women	
16–29	10.0	(50)	7.9	(39)	8.9	(89)
30–49	30.2	(197)	25.6	(170)	27.9	(366)
50–64	85.6	(401)	84.6	(433)	85.0	(833)
65–74	211.4	(356)	227.1	(559)	220.7	(915)
75 and over	316.2	(243)	409.0	(625)	378.0	(867)
All ages	66.7	(1247)	88.2	(1825)	78.0	(3071)

Source: Harris (1971:4–5).

found that about two-thirds of those over 60 years did not use their wheelchairs all the time, usually because they were ambulant indoors.

The Harris study has formed the basis for much subsequent thinking about disability and has played an important role in the planning and development of services. However, there are a number of important criticisms that can be levelled. Townsend suggested that the Harris study adopted too narrow a definition of disability and therefore grossly underestimated the numbers of disabled people in the population: 'disability itself might be best defined as inability to perform the activities, share in the relationships and play the roles which are customary for people of broadly the same age and sex in society' (Townsend, 1979:691). In operationalising his broader definition in his massive survey of poverty he concluded that there were three times as many handicapped people as Harris suggested. Table 2.2 illustrates the differences in numbers produced by these two surveys.

There are two points of clarification that need to be made. First, the Harris figure of 1 297 000 individuals with no handicap refers to people who have impairments but are not handicapped, at least according to this particular definition. Second, the Townsend figure of 2 890 000 people with little or no handicap includes 180 000 children between the ages 0–9. Children were specifically excluded from the Harris survey.

The figures produced by Harris have not always proved reliable in estimating the cost of introducing new benefits,

Table 2.2   *The disabled in Britain: two national surveys*

Harris, A. (1971)		Townsend (1979)	
Degree of handicap	Total numbers	Degree of incapacity	Total numbers
Very severe	161 000	Very severe	325 000
Severe	366 000	Severe	780 000
Appreciable	633 000	Appreciable	1 990 000
Minor	699 000	Some	3 915 000
No handicap	1 297 000	Little or none	2 890 000
Total	3 146 000	Total	9 900 000

nor indeed do the figures always match with data collected by government for other purposes. According to Jaehnig (in Boswell and Wingrove, 1974:449, n.2), upon the introduction of the attendance allowance it was estimated from the Harris survey that there were approximately 25 000 people entitled to it – yet in the first year alone there were more than 72 000 successful applicants. And Topliss points out:

> From the government survey in 1969 it was estimated there were 697 000 impaired men and women in the labour force or temporarily off sick or actively seeking work. Only 176 000 of these were classified as substantially handicapped by their impairments. On the other hand, there were in 1978 over half a million names on the Disabled Persons Employment Register, kept by the Employment Services Agency, and yet it was thought that only one third of those eligible to register in fact were registered. This would suggest that there are substantially more than the estimated 697 000 impaired people in the work force. (Topliss, 1979:48)

She went on to suggest that this discrepancy is 'undoubtedly due to the different definitions of disability employed', in that many people who may have few or minor functional limitations may nevertheless be severely handicapped in obtaining employment.

Functional definitions are still not acceptable to all, and Finkelstein suggests that these definitions still locate the causes of disability at the level of the individual, whereas 'The cause of handicap lies within the society which disadvantages impaired people . . . handicap is caused by having steps into buildings and not inability to walk' (in Finlay, 1978, app. 7). Finkelstein then proposes a reversal of the Harris terminology along the following lines:

> Firstly, that the cause of handicap lies within the society which disadvantages impaired people by taking no, or very little account of their physical condition and consequently does not provide the solutions, for example providing ramps for wheelchair users who are unable to walk up steps . . . Secondly, I suggest changing the definitions of the words handicap and disability around. In this way a person is disabled when he or she is socially prevented from full participation by the way society is arranged. (in Finlay, 1978, app. 7)

While there are very real and important criticisms of the Harris work, it did at least attempt to obtain the extent of the problems of disability looked at in a coherent and systematic way. Unfortunately, while the Harris survey recognised the social dimension of disability, it still attempted to utilise what remains an individual measure and to locate the problems of disability within the individual. Bury (1996) argues that this resulted in the identification of the consequences of disability but not in any greater financial compensation or consideration of disabled people's views. He suggests that:

> In part this arose from the continuing part that medicine played, within administrative circles, in adjudicating access to benefits. In order to tackle this problem, and provide new estimates of disability based on a broader definition, a new national study was commissioned by the OPCS in 1984, and several surveys, including one on children, were carried out between 1985 and 1988. The main purpose of this new initiative was to inform a review of social security in the disability field, and pave the way for such benefits to be based on a more systematic appreciation of the relational character of disability. (Bury, 1996:21)

These new surveys continued to make use of the World Health Organisation definitions of impairment, disability and handicap

Table 2.3   *Estimates of the numbers of disabled adults and children in Great Britain by severity category.*

Severity category	Adults	Children
10	210 000	34 000
9	365 000	25 000
8	396 000	31 000
7	486 000	46 000
6	545 000	38 000
5	708 000	43 000
4	704 000	43 000
3	750 000	48 000
2	840 000	19 000
1	1 198 000	33 000
Total	6 202 000	360 000

Sources: Martin *et al.* (1988) and Bone and Meltzer (1989).

but attempted to be more sensitive than their predecessors. This time the surveys produced ten categories of severity rather than the four used by Harris. Pen pictures of people who had been categorised were provided in the reports to illustrate the meaning of each of these. Table 2.3 shows the results of the surveys in terms of their estimations of adults and children into the different severity categories.

What is immediately apparent is that these surveys revealed twice as many disabled adults (6 202 000) as had Harris, and a further 360 000 disabled children. However, as Abberley (1992) has argued, if the people in the least severe categories (1–3), who would probably not have qualified for inclusion in Harris's 'impaired' category, were to be be removed then the total remains similar to that in the earlier study. One of the results of this is that the surveys underestimated the additional costs to individuals of disablement as their respondents were predominantly in the lower categories. In their own surveys of severely disabled adults the Disablement Income Group found the average extra weekly expenditure to be 58 per cent higher than the OPCS estimates (Abberley, 1992).

Martin *et al.* confirmed Harris's earlier findings concerning the prevalence of disability amongst different age groups (see Table 2.4), and as Bury (1996) argues they should be

Table 2.4 *Estimates of prevalence of disability among adults by age and severity category for men and women (cumulative rate per 1000 population)*

Severity category	Men, age group				Women, age group			
	16–59	60–74	75 and over	Total	16–59	60–74	75 and over	Total
10	1	5	21	3	1	4	45	6
9–10	3	17	64	9	4	18	102	17
8–10	6	31	107	16	8	31	154	28
7–10	10	46	150	24	13	50	224	42
6–10	14	62	191	32	19	73	293	58
5–10	20	87	250	45	28	106	369	78
4–10	27	117	309	58	36	136	431	97
3–10	34	155	369	73	44	172	495	115
2–10	41	207	442	92	51	213	561	135
1–10	56	283	533	121	64	264	631	161

Source: Martin *et al.* (1988:22, Table 3.7).

commended for not initially identifying the age of respondents and therefore not making the assumption that certain functional limitations were caused by old age and by implication not an impairment. The surveys confirmed that disability was far more prevalent in older age groups with almost 70 per cent being over 60 years.

However, the OPCS estimates were notably lower than the estimates of prevalence from the 1985 General Household Survey (GHS) in all age groups below 75 years. Martin *et al.* (1988) explain this by the design of their survey which only counted people if they were limited in specific activities, whereas the GHS counted limitations to any activity. The lower incidence in the GHS estimates after 75 years is accounted for by the probability that many older people might not perceive themselves as limited by illness, disability or infirmity, but by age and therefore would not have been counted by the GHS. Overall the 1985 General Household Survey suggests that there may be half as many more disabled adults as the OPCS surveys estimated, putting the total numbers of disabled adults at over 9.5 million.

There are clearly some key methodological and definitional problems in trying to estimate the prevalence of disability through functional definitions which is reinforced by the 1991 census which found yet another figure of 7 190 000 people in Great Britain with a 'limiting long-term illness'. The problem, however, is more than one of accuracy as Barnes states:

> this approach creates artificial distinctions and barriers between disabled people and the rest of society which, at best, prolong ignorance and misunderstanding and, at worst, nourish and sustain ancient fears and prejudices. (Barnes, 1991:25)

In an effort to provide consistency and minimise confusions over definitions and terminology, the World Health Organisation (WHO) commissioned Dr Philip Wood at Manchester University to expand upon the existing 'International Classification of Disease' to cover the consequences of long-term illness. The result 'The International Classification of Impairment, Disability and Handicap' (ICIDH) was published in 1980. Widely regarded as the most comprehensive catalogue of its kind, it has been used as a basis for government initiatives on disability in both the developed and developing world.

It is not inaccurate to say that the ICIDH has not been successful as a tool to classify disabled people and there have been very few studies which have managed to operationalise it properly. Even the United Nations in its recent study (Despouy, 1993) failed to make use of it. Consequently WHO is currently seeking to revise the whole scheme and to add a fourth, environmental dimension.

The WHO definitions that have informed the OPCS surveys conceive the social dimensions of disability as arising from the 'abnormality' of impairment. The argument of the social model of disability is that the causal relationship begins with the reactions of mainstream society to people with impairments that oppresses and excludes them. Part of this oppression is the imposition of an understanding of disability that blames the individual. Oliver (1990) has argued that this was clearly apparent in the face-to-face interviews within OPCS disability surveys. By re-wording some of the questions used by the researchers he demonstrates the way in which respondents were influenced to consider themselves as inadequate:

Questions from Survey of Disabled Adults – OPCS 1986

- What complaint causes your difficulty in holding, gripping or turning things?
- Are your difficulties in understanding people mainly due to a hearing problem?
- Do you have a scar, blemish or deformity which limits your daily activities?
- Have you attended a special school because of a long-term health problem or disability?
- Does your health problem / disability mean that you need to live with relatives or someone else who can look after you?

Alternative Questions – Oliver 1990

- What defects in the design of everyday equipment like jars, bottles or tins causes you difficulty in holding, gripping or turning them?
- Are your difficulties in understanding people mainly due to their inabilities to communicate with you?
- Do other people's reactions to any scar, blemish or deformity you may have, limit your daily activities?
- Have you attended a special school because of your education authority's policy of sending people with your health problem or disability to such places?
- Are community services so poor that you need to rely on relatives or someone else to provide you with the right level of personal assistance?

Bury (1996) is critical of this approach to the analysis of the OPCS surveys and points out their positive role in highlighting the predominance of chronic illnesses such as arthritis and hearing loss as causes of disability. He argues that this helps to explain not only the higher prevalence amongst older people but also the gender differences and goes on to to suggest that:

> no matter how justifiable the attempt is to influence the direction of the operation of welfare, and notably social security, away from medical adjudication, a full picture of

disablement in contemporary populations inevitably exposes its health and illness dimensions. From the viewpoint of everyday experience, therefore, different aspects of health and welfare needs may be relevant. Moreover, these dimensions have implications for different forms of intervention on the impairment, disability and handicap continuum. (Bury, 1996:22)

Both the criticisms from Oliver and Barnes and the support of Bury for the OPCS surveys have at their heart a concern for the impact of the research on the lives of disabled people. It is helpful in examining this to look at the ways in which research has been operationalised within social work. While the results of the Harris survey were being published, the Chronically Sick and Disabled Persons Act was making its way through Parliament. Its very first section stated:

It shall be the duty of every local authority having functions under section 29 of the National Assistance Act 1948 to inform themselves of the number of persons to whom that section applies within their area and of the need for the making by the authority of arrangements under that section for such persons.

So it was not just a matter of counting heads but also of making provision to meet need.

The main reason for including this section was not merely to identify the numbers of disabled people in particular local authority areas, for that could have been done by reference to the Harris survey which had analysed its data in this fashion, but rather to identify each disabled individual in a particular area. As Topliss and Gould (1981:90) put it, 'There can be no doubt, therefore, that the original intention of Alf Morris was that local authorities should identify, person by person, the handicapped individuals in their respective areas'. However, under guidance from the DHSS, local authorities were directed towards making assessments of numbers rather than attempting to identify specifically every disabled individual. All local authorities complied with this duty either by carrying out house-to-house surveys, sample surveys or using other methods.

Knight and Warren have summarised the findings of these surveys and suggested:

Most of the CSDP [Chronically Sick and Disabled Persons Act] surveys found that the crude prevalence rate for all impaired and handicapped people living in the community was from 40 to 70 people per 1000 of the population of all ages, i.e. from 4% to 7% of the population were found to be physically impaired. Between one third and one half of these were handicapped, i.e. experienced significant disadvantage, in one way or another, by their impairment and just over one tenth (or nearly 1% of the whole population) were very severely or severely handicapped. The presence of impairment and handicap increased markedly with age. Fewer than 1% of the population aged less than 16 years were impaired, about 3% of those aged from 16–64 years, about 18% of those aged from 65 to 74 years and from 40% to 50% of those aged 75 years or more. It follows from this that the majority of disabled people are elderly and many are very old and, because of the longer life of women compared to men, most disabled people in the older age groups are women (after the age of 75 years two thirds or more of disabled people are likely to be women). (Knight and Warren, 1978:68–9)

From this it will be seen that these surveys provide a picture of disability, at least in terms of age structure, gender and severity of disability, at the local level which is broadly similar to the national picture found by Harris. However, in numerical terms the numbers of disabled people on local authority registers in England in 1980 was 900 669. Thus it is clear that social services departments had located only one in three disabled people, at least according to the Harris estimate of numbers.

Nowhere in the Chronically Sick and Disabled Persons Act 1970 was the idea of a register mentioned, but as the keeping of a register of disabled people was made a requirement of the National Assistance Act 1948, many local authorities decided that keeping one was the way to meet their duty under section 1. As Phelan (1979) puts it, 'Section 1 was hailed as the master key to social provision for people with handicap'. There are problems in keeping registers, however. First, some people may feel that inclusion on a register is an invasion of privacy and may be stigmatising. While all sorts of actions may be taken to reduce the stigma, it cannot be got rid of entirely as these registers represent the control and dominance of the administrative model of welfare which as Finkelstein has argued, assumes 'that disability means social death necessitating interventions by able-bodied professionals and lay workers who then "administer" the cure or care solutions' (Finkelstein, 1991:27). Second, it is difficult to keep registers up to date and in line with changing circumstances and capabilities of those registered. Finally, as has already been pointed out, Warren *et al.* (1979) showed that registers are likely to be extremely inaccurate (by up to 30 per cent or more). Even with the help of new technologies and its promise of efficiency in record keeping, the level of accuracy has changed little and the problems of updating information remain (Glastonbury, 1995). The most telling criticism of registration, however, is that there is only a tenuous link between it and the provision of services. The following situation is described by Topliss and Gould:

> None of the services for handicapped individuals is conditional upon the recipient being first recorded on a local authority register. Neither is the entry of a person's name on the register any guarantee that he or she will receive any service at all. It is true that more of those who are registered are in receipt of services than those who are not registered, but this is chiefly because application and receipt of a service identifies a person as handicapped and his or her case is then recorded. In other words, it is the fact that a service has been asked for and given that leads to entry on the register for many disabled people, rather than the other way round. There is certainly still a good deal of ignorance on the part of disabled people about services provided by the local authority for which they may be eligible, but merely registering a person as disabled does little or nothing to broaden his knowledge of services that could assist him. The dissemination of information to disabled

people about services can be, and usually is quite independent of any register. (Topliss and Gould, 1981:100–1)

Finally, then, the criteria for registration offers considerable discretionary powers to those doing the registering, both in terms of the resources available in a given area and the personal whims of those undertaking the registration process. Satyamurti found examples of this:

> Criteria for registration were laid down, but these criteria left a certain amount of room for interpretation which made it possible for there to be a considerable degree of variation in practice, both between individual social workers and, probably more importantly, between area teams, as to the kind of criteria laid down. Other teams, however, took as their criteria not so much the characteristics of the client concerned, as considerations about what services would be available to that client if he/she were registered, which would not otherwise be available. Thus in Area X, for instance, it was common practice for social workers to register clients, particularly the elderly, as physically handicapped on such grounds as shortness of breath or arthritic pain, in order that they could then arrange for the client to have a holiday to which otherwise he/she would not be entitled. Social workers would vie with each other in a joking way as to how little in the way of physical impairment they could get away with. (Satyamurti, 1981:37)

Despite the clear problems that had been identified, the keeping of registers of disabled children became a requirement under Schedule 2 of the Children Act 1989. Middleton (1995) makes the same point about these being an infringement of civil liberties as Barnes has made of the large-scale surveys of disability. It amounts to a process of problematising all disabled children in a way that would be totally unacceptable if it were any other identifiable group of the population. Middleton also makes the point that where local authorities attempt to defend this practice they do so on the grounds that it will help their planning of services. This she describes as:

... chilling in the extreme, since it suggests that they have some preconceived notion of what the future holds in terms of needs of disabled children, and adults, for services. Given the apparent lack of imagination of many local authorities this can only mean preprogramming children either for day care of for its current substitute of everlasting segregated education. (Middleton, 1995:7)

The problem of registration for social work, particularly when viewed from a social model of disability, is a false one. It starts from the assumption, built into the Chronically Sick and Disabled Persons Act, that all disabled people have special needs and that statutory provision should be made to meet them. The resource implications of such a view have become apparent and need not be dwelt upon here. However, it is the assumption that all disabled people should be identified in order to meet their needs that is false.

It has been variously estimated that perhaps as many as three in four disabled people may not wish to be known to social services or have any needs that statutory provision might meet. One study, based on a survey of Remploy employees (Owen, 1981), found that only 40 per cent of those interviewed had actually used the services of a social worker. Given that registers appear to identify only one-third of disabled people, it is clear that the idea of providing a comprehensive service for all disabled people has proved unattainable. In addition the underlying assumption locates the problem within the individual and fails to take into account the way the physical and social environments are disabling. Services are therefore geared to the problems of individual limitations rather than to alleviating the restricting effects of physical and social environments. Social services departments and social workers, then, most of whom have regarded registration as a crucial issue, have in fact been operating in the wrong area. Phelan makes a clarion call to social workers:

Transform the war memorial of Registration into a roll of honour, put it on display and have a page turned daily to a fanfare of trumpets. For the benefit of citizens with handicaps let us explode the myth of registration, exploit its meaning and clear the way for counting to lead to caring. (Phelan, 1979)

The social work task in this particular area is thus not to identify and register impaired individuals; it is rather (i) to identify ways in which disabilities are imposed upon impairments with a view to remediation, and (ii) to provide a flexible and accessible service to meet such individual needs as may arise. It is for planners and policy-makers, not social workers, to identify the likely extent of such needs. Of course, some will say that this is all very well, but central government at present allocates funds to local authorities on the basis of head counts, but there is no reason why local authorities should not suggest that this is an inappropriate way to proceed, and that alternative ways of estimating and meeting needs should be explored. Sutherland, for example, suggests that new definitions of disability need to be developed:

> The most useful basis for such a definition is the fact of stigmatisation itself. If we make no attempt to create a definition based upon some type of physical incapacity, but simply define this group as consisting of all people who are stigmatised or discriminated against on the basis of their physical condition, we have an extremely practical rule of thumb definition. (Sutherland, 1981:20)

Whether a definition based on stigma would prove adequate is perhaps debatable, but it is certainly clear that any definitions need to move away from personal physical incapacity or functional limitation as their base-line.

Self-definitions

It is not just individual disabled people like Finkelstein and Sutherland who are articulating different definitions of disability, but a growing number of disability organisations are also demanding the right to define the problems faced by their own members. More will be said of this later but it is worth noting at this point that the inaugural meeting of Disabled

People's International, a congress representing disabled people from over 50 countries, rejected the International Classification of Impairments, Disabilities and Handicaps (World Health Organisation, 1980) on the grounds that it was too closely allied to medical and individual definitions of disability.

Self-definitions are not only important at the level of the disabled individual. Professionals have often been reluctant to accept a disabled person's own definition and have used terms like 'denial' and 'disavowal' to account for contradictions between definitions. The assumption that has usually followed from this is that it is the disabled person who is mistaken or misguided and the professional who is correct. It logically follows from this perception of a given situation that the social work task is to facilitate a more realistic assessment of the situation by disabled persons themselves.

What in practice this may amount to is the social worker imposing the professional definition upon the disabled person, and it is certainly true that the only way to gain access to certain benefits and services is to 'act disabled'. However, as Blaxter's study showed, in situations where professional and self-definitions conflict, this was much more likely to give rise to long-term problems than when these definitions were in accord: 'One of the circumstances in which the problems of adjustment and rehabilitation were very likely was when the patient's own view of his condition differed from that of his doctors' (Blaxter, 1980:221).

The problem for professionals generally, and for social workers in particular, is not working out the correct or right definition of disability, for part of the argument here is that there is no such thing. Definitions depend upon a number of factors, some of which have already been identified and some of which have not. Albrecht and Levy argue that definitions of disability are socially constructed and such social constructions often reflect vested professional interests:

Certainly it is in the interest of medical professionals, hospitals, nursing homes, and medical supply companies to find treatable, chronic disabilities. Yet, the disabilities identified, discovered, and treated may reflect professional and occupational exigencies rather than actual consumer need. For these reasons, *disabilities can be seen as socially constructed entities regardless of their physiological bases*. (Albrecht and Levy, 1981:21, our emphasis)

Thus social workers need to recognise that disability is a social construction and not necessarily a fixed physical entity, and need to plan their strategies of intervention accordingly. Some of the ways in which they might do this are considered in the following chapters.

3

The Causes of Impairment and the Creation of Disability

The distinction between individual and social dimensions of disability already referred to are also important in discussing the causes of both impairment (individual limitation) and disability (socially imposed restriction). From an individual/ medical view the main causes of impairment can be seen in Table 3.1.

Commenting on previous such studies, Taylor has suggested that this approach is entirely justified in that the major causes of impairments are diseases of various kinds. It follows from this that 'Unlike the case of most instances of mental handicap, there is a significant medical contribution to be made within the overall pattern of support for physically disabled individuals' (Taylor, 1977:10). In short, most impairments are caused by disease, doctors cure diseases, and even where they cannot be cured medical intervention will often control symptoms. Therefore, doctors have an important, if not crucial, role to play. The question of the relevance of medical knowledge for social work intervention will be discussed later in the chapter.

It is also argued that these diseases are 'residual'; and that their increased incidence is a result of two factors, increased life expectancy and the growing numbers of elderly people in the population. A consequence of this view is the assumption that these diseases are 'degenerative' and largely a product of the age structure of the population. According to Doyal:

The new 'disease burden' consists largely of the so-called 'degenerative' diseases, such as cancer, heart disease, arthritis

Table 3.1 *Frequency of complaints in International Classification of Diseases groups causing disability by severity category: all adults*

| ICD groups | Percentage of disabled with complaint in each ICD group (severity category) | | | | | All groups |
	1–2	3–4	5–6	7–8	9–10	1–10
Infections	1	1	1	1	1	1
Neoplasms	1	1	2	3	6	2
Endocrine	1	2	3	4	5	2
Blood	0	1	1	0	1	1
Mental	11	17	19	19	25	16
Nervous system	4	10	16	24	38	14
Eye	18	19	24	27	32	22
Ear	39	34	35	37	32	36
Circulatory	18	21	21	20	15	20
Respiratory	12	14	14	13	10	13
Digestive	4	5	7	8	5	6
Genito-urinary	1	3	4	5	8	3
Skin	1	1	1	1	2	1
Musculo-skeletal	35	45	53	57	44	45
Congenital	0	1	1	0	0	0
Other/vague	4	6	8	9	11	6

Note: Percentages do not add to 100 as some people have more than one condition.

Sources: Adapted from Martin *et al.* (1988, Table 4.10, p. 34) and Martin *et al.* (1989, Table 2.21, p. 9).

and diabetes, all of which now kill and cripple many more people than they did in the past. In 1975, approximately 26 per cent of deaths in Britain occurred from cerebrovascular disease, 20 per cent as a result of cancer, and 4.5 per cent as a result of chronic bronchitis, emphysema or asthma. In addition, of course, many more people are becoming chronically ill for longer periods in their lives than they did in the past. (Doyal, 1980:59)

The diseases causing death and disability are very similar, but whereas Taylor sees the prospects of prevention as limited and the medical profession as the appropriate agency for dealing with the causes and consequences of such conditions, Doyal has an alternative view more in accord with Finkelstein's social definition of disability. It could be argued that while Finkelstein suggests that disability has social causes, Doyal sees impairment as having social causes also.

Using the work of Powles (1973) Doyal argues that these degenerative diseases occur almost exclusively in advanced industrial societies and, regardless of their individual causes, they result from the fact that the environment to which humans are biologically adapted has changed fundamentally. The living conditions of advanced industrial societies produce diseases of 'maladaptation'. The implications of this view differ from those derived from the view of Taylor, in that if the causes of these diseases are ultimately environmental (social) rather than individual, then perhaps the medical profession is not the crucial agency that should be involved. In short, if these diseases are the consequence of a dysfunction between human beings and the environment, then it is to the material environment that programmes of treatment (or prevention) should be directed. Indeed, some writers, notably Illich (1975), have suggested that the disappearance of a number of diseases such as typhoid, cholera, polio and tuberculosis is solely due to changes in the material environment and the role of medicine has been irrelevant or even positively harmful. He develops his argument through usage of the term 'iatrogenesis', by which he means 'doctor-induced illness', which he defines as 'illness which would not have come about unless sound and professionally recommended treatment had been applied'.

Prevention

A major reason for considering the causes of both impairment and disability is that it raises the possibility of prevention. As Albrecht and Levy put it:

> The major causes of mortality and morbidity today – heart disease, cancer, stroke, diabetes and accidents – can be prevented partially by changes in the environment and lifestyle. That is why the Surgeon General of the United States advocates altered health practices in terms of smoking, overweight, drinking alcoholic beverages, hours of sleep, regu-

larity of eating breakfast, eating between meals and physical activity . . . Disability and the costs of rehabilitation could be partially controlled if those precipitating events that are preventable were eliminated. To avoid blaming the victim, preventative efforts should be directed at the industries and governmental agencies that promote disability-causing behavior rather than by merely faulting those individuals who become disabled. (Albrecht and Levy, 1981:26–7)

However, the term 'prevention' as used by the medical profession is not necessarily the same thing as the concept of 'prevention' used by social workers. Leonard (1966) attempted to distinguish between three levels, which he calls primary, secondary and tertiary. For him primary intervention is aimed at preventing the causes of certain events, secondary intervention is aimed at preventing the immediate effects of events, and tertiary intervention is aimed at preventing the consequences of these events. This threefold distinction is very similar to the classifications of disability produced by Harris and Finkelstein discussed in the previous chapter. The ideas discussed so far can be summarised in the form of Table 3.2.

This perspective therefore sees the medical profession and health educators as being largely responsible for primary prevention: that is, reducing the numbers of disabled babies being born, providing information about the prevention of accidents at work, and so on. Secondary prevention, that is, the reduction of the personal limitations that may be imposed by impairments, falls to rehabilitation staff in particular. Tertiary prevention, that is, the reduction of socially-imposed restrictions upon impaired individuals, forms a large part of the social work task in working with people with disabilities though, as Holdsworth (1991) has pointed out, this also requires the support of the social work institutions and society.

Leonard (1966:12) has suggested in respect of social work generally, 'Much of social work has concentrated, necessarily, on tertiary intervention; for example, the intervention involved in the whole field of the care of adults and children in residential institutions, foster homes and hostels'. Leonard's description of the social work task with disabled people contains an interesting contradiction which illustrates the argument of

Table 3.2 *Definitions and the scope for intervention*

Professional intervention	Individual model (Harris, 1971; Martin et al., 1988; Taylor, 1977)	Social model (Finkelstein, in Finlay, 1978)	Type of prevention (Leonard, 1966)
Medical profession and health education	**Impairment**	**Impairment** (Treatment and care)	**Primary**
Paramedics and rehabilitation staff, e.g. OTs, physios	**Disability**	**Impairment** (Therapy)	**Secondary**
Social workers, politicians, pressure groups	**Handicap**	**Disability**	**Tertiary**

this book. If on the one hand intervention at a tertiary level involves the reduction of socially-imposed restrictions upon impaired individuals, it follows that this would amount to the prevention of disability, thereby making it a form of primary intervention from a social-model perspective. However, the example given by Leonard of care within institutions forms one of the more obviously disabling responses of society towards people with impairments rather than a preventative one. What is preventative, therefore, is clearly relative to the perspective from which the issue of disability is being analysed.

From an individual-model perspective, social work has probably been involved at the primary and secondary levels also, in providing antenatal advice to pregnant clients or in helping to locate rehabilitation services. These are also not without their problems in terms of the way Leonard sees them. It is only from an individual-model analysis that assumes a eugenicist concept of 'normality' that it can be concluded, for example, that aborting a foetus which is impaired is preventative of disability. From a social-model perspective the disability is caused by the reactions of the society into which the child is born. As Dona Avery put it when describing how she had been expected by hospital staff to follow the five stages of the Kubler-

Ross model (Denial; Anger; Bargaining; Depression and Acceptance):

> I have seen a 5th stage, and it is not Acceptance or Hope of a Cure. It is learning that an unborn perfect child was one conceived by society, not me, and that the actual child I *was* gifted with is perfectly fine. (Avery, 1997)

Equally, the organisation of rehabilitation services can be viewed as helpful in functional terms or it may be seen in quite a different way:

> Our first concern is that disabled people are faced with impossible social, financial, housing and environmental difficulties, and are then offered a piecemeal welfare system of professionals and services to help them adjust to and cope with their unacceptable circumstances. (Brechin and Liddiard, 1981:2).

Traditionally however, social work has been essentially concerned with the tertiary level within an individual model of disability. Although there may now be considerable administrative limitations placed upon those who are employed in highly regimented organisations as care managers, it remains that intervention at this level holds out the best starting point for changing to work within a social model of disability. It is necessary therefore to explore the range of knowledge and skills needed to carry out this task.

Medical knowledge and the social work task

One immediate question posed by this conceptualisation of the social work task concerns the question of how much knowledge of medical conditions social workers actually need. In suggesting that it is the social rather than the individual/medical model within which social workers should operate, it does not logically follow that they should have no knowledge of medical conditions. Indeed, without such knowledge it may well be impossible to consider the personal, interpersonal or social consequences for the client concerned. Such knowledge may be acquired from other professionals or through reference books of various kinds. *Get Help* by Halliburton and Quelch (1981) is a particularly useful example. However, in most cases the major source of such knowledge is the disabled person. Thus one young social worker, when allocated to work with a tetraplegic woman, approached her new client by telling her that she knew nothing about tetraplegia but was willing to learn. The worker and client thereby agreed to spend a complete day together from the time before the tetraplegic woke up until after she fell asleep in bed. The social worker learned more about tetraplegia from that particular experience than ever she could have done from books or other sources, and as a consequence was able to provide the client with satisfactory service.

It is important to extract other aspects from the medical facts: whether the condition is visible or non-visible, whether it is static or progressive, congenital or acquired, whether the impairment is sensory or physical, will all have important effects upon the personal, interpersonal and social consequences of particular impairments. Hicks spells this out in the case of visual impairment:

> Because of the inabilities to acquire information through sight and to make eye contact with other people, the visually handicapped, and particularly the functionally blind, may encounter relationship and sexual problems which are not common to other disabilities. These problems differ for those whose visual impairment is congenital (from birth or infancy) or adventitious (occurring after some visual concepts have been formed). They apply to initial encounters, to the range of potential partners, to sexual relationships and they have clear implications for education and counselling and for professional relationships with the client. (in Brechin *et al.*, 1981:79)

What is being suggested, for visual impairment in particular and for all disabilities in general, is that such aspects are more important for the social worker than to know whether the impairment was caused by glaucoma, cataracts or retinitis pigmentosa.

Disability, then, is neither simply an individual misfortune nor a social problem: it is a relationship between the impaired individual and the restrictions imposed upon him by society. This relationship is defined by Finkelstein: 'society disables people with different physical impairments. The cause, then, of disability, is the social relationships which take little or no account of people who have physical impairments' (in Brechin *et al.*, 1981:34). Disability is thus a relationship between individual impairments and the social restrictions imposed by social organisation.

A framework for intervention

For the social worker to utilise this idea of disability as a relationship, some way of linking the individual and the social is needed. One such attempt has been made through development of the concept of 'career', which originally developed in American sociology (Becker, 1963; Goffman, 1963) but later came to be used on both sides of the Atlantic in discussions of disability (Safilios-Rothschild, 1970; Blaxter, 1980). Carver has provided a comprehensive definition of the concept in relation to disability:

A 'career in disability' refers to the course of progress through life of any disabled person insofar as he encounters problems or handicapping conditions related in any way to his disabilities. A person's progress may be affected in relation to his working life, but not his domestic or wider social life – or vice versa – but this would be likely to happen only if the disability were a minor and limited one, since for most people all aspects of life tend to be inter-related. It may be affected in practical ways and/or in the ways he thinks about himself or others. This concept of career is a broadly comprehensive one and implies that the individual is actively and repeatedly involved in the definition of his own problems and in the search for solutions, and like any other career, it will comprise a succession of interactions with his environment, both physical and social. A career in disability may in principle come to an end when all impairment-related problems have been solved; but in the case of enduring disability fresh problems may arise at any time and it is wiser to assume that the individual's career may persist from the onset of disability until the end of his life. (Carver, 1982:90)

Thus in working with individuals the concept of career provides a link with social structure and offers the social worker the possibility of conceptualising disability as a social relationship. On its own the idea of a 'career' will provide a useful basis for short-term or crisis intervention in that support and help may be needed when a career in disability begins. But for some people with disabilities longer-term involvement may be necessary.

In order fully to make use of the concept of 'career' it needs to be harnessed to the notion of 'life-cycle events': that is, that there are key transition stages in life through which everyone passes, such as birth, starting and leaving school, puberty, going to work, marriage, retirement and death. These transition stages are often marked by uncertainty as individuals move from one role or status to another, and this can give rise to adjustment problems both for the individuals themselves, and for family, friends, peers and so on. Disabled people will also move through key life-cycle events, though disability may exacerbate some of the problems involved and enhance the need for professional intervention. For example, anxious parents may well seek to help their disabled offspring at a childhood stage well into the period when disabled people feel they should be treated as adults.

From other social scientific research it is possible to predict certain occurrences at particular stages in the life-cycle. For example, poverty is more likely to occur when a family is bringing up young children and around the point of retirement; personal relationships are often fraught around the time of puberty; unemployment can be particularly severe during adolescence; and family crises may occur during the early years of marriage when parents are adapting to having young children in the home. It is possible to link together the concepts of 'career' and 'life-cycle events' in diagrammatic form as shown in Figure 3.1.

The first column in Figure 3.1 provides a chronological listing of the ages at which life-cycle events occur and these events

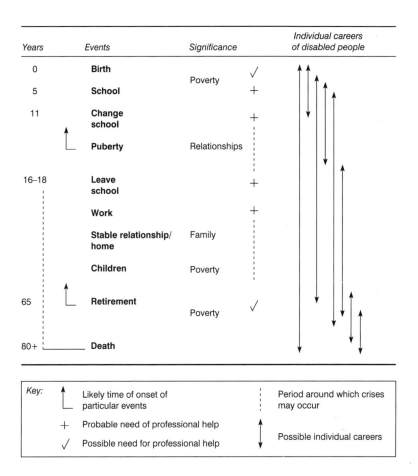

Years	Events	Significance	Individual careers of disabled people
0	**Birth**	Poverty	✓
5	**School**		+
11	**Change school**		+
	Puberty	Relationships	
16–18	**Leave school**		+
	Work		+
	Stable relationship/ home	Family	
	Children	Poverty	
65	**Retirement**	Poverty	✓
80+	**Death**		

Key:			
↑⌐	Likely time of onset of particular events	┊	Period around which crises may occur
+	Probable need of professional help	↑↓	Possible individual careers
✓	Possible need for professional help		

Figure 3.1 *Disabled careers and life-cycle events*

are then listed in the second column. The third column then provides some indication of the kind of events that may occur and the need for intervention. The fourth column plots a number of possible 'disabled careers'. This final column indicates that disability can occur at any particular point in the life-cycle, and can also end, sometimes by the provision of a cure, and more often by early or premature death. The point of the diagram is to sensitise the social worker to the 'disability relationship' and the number of possible factors which may be involved. Which of them is important and should serve as a target of intervention will be for the worker, in full discussion with the client, to determine. For example, one disabled woman experienced severe emotional difficulties during her adolescence but the social work support she received was solely geared towards her impairment. She now realises that her impairment was unrelated to her emotional disturbance, which was part of the normal process of growing up experienced by many girls.

As we have mentioned previously, Creek *et al.* (1987) made use of the concept of significant life events in their study of the social implications of spinal injury. This was argued on the basis of the inadequacy of the personal tragedy theory with its behavioural analysis of how individuals are expected to react to the onset of disability. Quoting from Silver and Wortman they put the case for this approach:

> Our review of the available literature suggests that a great deal of variability exists in individual reactions to negative life events, both within a particular life crisis and across different crises. We have found little reliable evidence to indicate that people go through stages of emotional responses following an undesirable life event. We have also reviewed a substantial body of evidence suggesting that a large minority of victims of aversive life events experience distress or disorganisation long after recovery might be expected. Current theoretical models of reactions to aversive outcomes cannot account for the variety of responses that appear. (Silver and Wortman quoted in Creek *et al.*, 1987:20–1)

This means that social workers need to view the concept of a 'disabled career' not as predetermined but as entirely individual. While the causes of disability lie in the social reactions to impairment, the ways in which any individual might then react to that process or to the onset of impairment will be determined by their own unique set of experiences and circumstances. The social worker therefore needs to understand the actions of each person in terms of its subjective meaning to that individual – it is an interactionist rather than behavioural understanding that is required.

It is necessary now to say something about the applicability of this scheme to the environment of social work practice. With limited resources, pressures on time from other cases, departmental management not sympathetic to this kind of work, and so on, most social workers are unlikely to have the luxury of planning long-term intervention in working with disabled people and their families. A properly planned long-term intervention strategy may not be a luxury but is economically justifiable in that planned intervention can be preventative and alleviate the need for more costly crisis intervention at some later stage. For example, some people with multiple sclerosis end up in residential care by the time they reach middle age, not because of the consequences of the progress of the disease, but because the caring relationship in which they are involved breaks down. Consistent, planned support could well prevent such breakdowns occurring.

Assessment

Involved in intervention strategies of whatever kind is the need for an assessment of the problem or problems. According to Bell and Klemz:

> In social services departments, the purpose of assessing the needs of physically handicapped clients is to bring to them the appropriate services which councils provide and to advise on other services that may be required. These can be services in terms of people, such as social workers or home-helps, or in terms of practical aid, such as provision of aids to daily living, adaptations, holidays, day care, etc. (Bell and Klemz, 1981:117)

More recently with the implementation of the NHS and Community Care Act 1990, the focus has moved from the consideration of services that are provided by councils to a needs-led approach to assessment. This was enshrined in the government's white paper *Caring for People* (Department of Health, 1989) and in the subsequent policy and practice guidance (Social Services Inspectorate, 1991a, b) which requires that social

workers and other assessors of need do not simply consider a
person's eligibility for an existing service, but look at what
services may have to be purchased or provided in order to
enable that individual to live more independently. The implementation of this needs-led approach was heralded with
criticisms of the service-led approach. In his foreword to Ellis'
study of user and carer participation in assessment, the chief
inspector of the Social Services Inspectorate likened the latter to the methods of Procrustes:

> Its findings are perhaps not unexpected to those familiar
> with the extraordinary pressures under which social services
> departments must work. Their assessment procedures are
> rather more sophisticated than those of the Greek robber
> Procrustes, 'who placed all who fell into his hands upon an
> iron bed. If they were longer than the bed he cut off the
> overhanging parts, if shorter he stretched them till they
> fitted it.' Even so the report demonstrates how the workers'
> preconceptions of policy, resources and values precluded
> that dialogue with users and carers which should be the
> foundation of joint assessment. Occupations which trade in
> non-judgementalism are shown to be as moralistic in their
> approach as any lay person. The ways in which some workers
> discouraged 'dependency' should impress the most fervent
> advocate of Victorian values, and shows that the spirit of
> the Poor Law is alive and kicking nearly 50 years after its
> official internment. (Utting in Ellis, 1993:3)

However, the introduction of a needs-led system of assessment has not been seen by all as the solution to the ills of
the past. Sapey (1993) argued that the NHS and Community
Care Act 1990 is simply the continuation of an ideological
tradition within social policy that started with the Poor Law
of 1601 in that it maintains that it is local authorities, rather
than disabled people, who know best what is needed by the
latter. In this sense it is hardly surprising that Utting should
find those values being implemented within social services
departments, but he is remiss to blame solely the practice of
the individuals employed when the policy structure itself demands such behaviour of them. Morris (1993) also questions

the meaning behind the rhetoric of the Act and the subsequent statements from local authorities:

> A number of Community Care Plans include statements about a commitment to enabling people to live independent lives. All these pronouncements, made by both politicians and professionals, are compatible with the independent living movement's assertion that disability is a civil rights issue, and that both central and local government policy should be concerned with removing the barriers to disabled people's full participation in society.
>
> However, this compatibility is actually a superficial one. The aim of independent living is held back by an ideology at the heart of community care policies, which does not recognise the civil rights of disabled people but instead considers them to be dependent people in need of care.
>
> (Morris, 1993:38)

Thompson (1993) also has doubts about the model of disability that lies behind the community care experiment:

> The current emphasis on 'care management' as a key part of the development of community care also retains the influence of the medical model, for example in the assumption that the professional experts know best what the needs of disabled people are. (Thompson, 1993:114)

The problems here are twofold. First we need to be able to distinguish between the rhetoric and reality of assessment policies and second, we need to ensure that assessments accurately reflect the needs of the client concerned, and not professional commitment, consciously or unconsciously, to one or other model or view of the world. Rowlings captures the second dilemma in discussing assessments of older people:

> The ... identification of the more obvious practical needs should also provide reliable information as to the presence or otherwise of additional emotional or relationship problems for which social work help may be appropriate. Not every client will require or want social work support and

certainly the provision of social service should not be dependent upon a social work recommendation. Nor is it feas-
ible or even desirable that every client referred for social
service also receives a separate assessment to see if social
work help is appropriate. (Rowlings, 1981:65–6)

This dilemma is equally true in assessment of disabled people,
and testament to the fact that social workers often get it wrong
can be found in Shearer:

> Understanding is meant to be part of the stock-in-trade of
> the social worker. They may have plenty of it but little prac-
> ticality: 'They are all very nice and sympathetic', says one
> middle-aged woman with cerebral palsy who lives with her
> now ageing mother. 'They will come and talk for hours.
> Then they go back and make long duplicated reports and
> nothing happens unless we keep on and on making a nuis-
> ance of ourselves.' Or they may not seem to understand at
> all. So a man who contacted his local social services office
> to seek help with getting his ceiling painted was treated
> instead to a lengthy visit which had to do with the need
> the social worker saw for him to come to terms with the
> fact that he had, some years ago, broken his spine. So a
> woman who quite badly wanted to discuss the particular strains
> of living with a disability that fluctuated in the restrictions
> it imposed was treated instead to a bright homily about the
> different bath aids now on the market. (Shearer, 1981a:113)

While the problems of poor assessment are easy to identify
it is perhaps more difficult to locate a particular model for
good practice. Sapey and Hewitt (1991) have argued that social workers and other social services personnel stand between
disabled people and their rights derived from various welfare
enactments. Because the provision of services is dependent
on the local authority assessment of need, this places the assessors of that need in the position not simply of gatekeeping
scarce resources, but of sanctioning the rights to services pre-
scribed by parliament. They go on to suggest that if assessments are to be needs-led they must also be undertaken by
the disabled person. Self-assessment, while posing a financial

nightmare to budget-holders, has the advantage of making clear the separation between need and the ability or willingness of any particular agency to meet that need. Doyal and Gough (1991) describe the professional assessment of need as a 'colonialist' approach in that it involves one group of experts determining what is best for another less powerful group of people. They argue for an objective and universal approach to the notion of needs and suggest that one of the principal benefits of this is to clearly separate the arguments over what human needs exist from the issue of how and to what extent any society may be willing to meet those needs. Self-assessment is also promoted by CCETSW:

> Self-assessment should be central to the assessment process and subsequent planning and evaluation should start from the same stand-point; in other words, disabled people are the best definers of their own needs. (Stevens, 1991:19)

Middleton has some concerns that the idea that disabled people always know best is also a 'simplistic rhetoric' that 'not only represent an avoidance of responsibility by professional helpers, but can be deeply disempowering for people who find themselves in new situations and need help' (Middleton, 1997: 73). For her, assessment is a four-stage process of:

1. Establishing a working relationship;
2. Data collection;
3. Analysis;
4. Planning.

However, she emphasises that assessment must also be more than a one-to-one activity that comes up with a plan:

> If assessment is to be a purposeful activity, it has to be more than that. Assessment is the art of managing competing demands, and negotiating the most reasonable outcome. It means steering between the clashing rocks of organisational demand; legislative dictates; limited resources; political and personal agendas. It includes having to keep one's feet in an inter-agency setting when the ground beneath

them is constantly shifting. It is about making sense of the situation as a whole, and working out the best way to achieve change. (Middleton, 1997:3–4)

A similar concern, though from a different starting point, is raised by Brechin and Liddiard about the relationship between professional and client and the extent to which the client is able to participate:

> It can be argued that, in making assessments, professionals are basically gathering information in order to clarify their understanding or model of what is going on in the same way as anyone might. Where there may be a difference is in the extent to which professionals formalise, condense and standardise the information gathering processes. By virtue of their training they have acquired certain preconstructed models which have been tried and tested already, and these they will attempt to use first to make sense of each new situation.
>
> By the same token, however, in developing a specialised focus, in attempting to maintain objectivity, and in trying to operate economically, professionals have a tendency to narrow the scope of their assessment. The individual involved, on the other hand, may be overwhelmed by an abundance of first hand information regarding all aspects of his/her life experiences and may find it quite hard to disentangle critical factors. If these two assessment procedures could be combined, the possibility of reaching a more balanced view would seem to be considerably increased. (Brechin and Liddiard, 1981:38–9)

There are good arguments, therefore, for the involvement of service-users in the assessment of their need for those services and this is a principle that appears to be enshrined in the guidance to implementing the National Health Service and Community Care Act 1990 (Social Services Inspectorate, 1991a, b). While the government chose not to implement Section 3 of the Disabled Persons (Services, Consultation and Representation) Act 1986 which formalised the rights of disabled people to be consulted and for their views to be taken into account by social service authorities, they approved the guidance issued by the Social Services Inspectorate and the Social Work Services Group (Scotland) that stated:

Enabling partnership with users and carers

The fundamental aim of community care is to promote the independence of individuals, so that they are able to live as normal lives as possible. Care management, as the process through which users gain access to services, should reinforce, not undermine, that aim.

Because practitioners and their managers control access to resources, the relationship will never be totally equal – but the present imbalance can be corrected by sharing information more openly and by encouraging users and carers, or their representatives, to take a full part in decision making.

The contribution of carers should be formally recognised in new procedures for care management and assessment. Because the interests of users and carers may not coincide, both parties should be given the opportunity of separate consultation with an assessing practitioner. If necessary, carers should be offered a separate assessment of their own needs. (Social Services Inspectorate, 1991b:16)

While the intent to involve disabled people is evident in this statement, it is also ambiguous and clearly retains the ideology of the individual model in its concern for the conflicts that may exist with the views and needs of carers. The failure to conceptualise disability as a social construct leads to this position where the needs of disabled people are seen as dependent on, and possibly subsidiary to, those of carers and precisely reinvents the helper-helped relationship identified by Finkelstein (1980). When we look at the way in which need itself is defined within care management the dominance of the individual model becomes obvious.

A care-management training package from the main social work trade union NALGO, specifically argued against placing too much value on the views of service-users. Meteyard (1992), while acknowledging the problems of paternalism and subjectivity associated with normative assessments of needs, nevertheless equates felt needs with 'wants' and argues for the use of the former in relation to community care, supporting his case with negative examples of drug addiction in which felt needs are damaging. By associating the demands of community care service-users with those of drug-users, he diminishes the value of felt needs and yet purports to be working from a value-base of empowerment. This position was reinforced by the government guidance which defined needs as 'the requirements of individuals to enable them to achieve, maintain or restore an acceptable level of social independence or quality of life, *as defined by the particular care agency or authority*' (our emphasis) (Social Services Inspectorate, 1991a:14). As Morris (1993) has pointed out, there is a gap between the rhetoric and reality in community care policies.

From a social-model perspective, the idea that assessment should be empowering seems clear and receives a lot of support, both in terms of the involvement of disabled people as full participants within the process of assessment, but also in terms of the outcomes. Morris (1997a) focuses on the skills required by individual practitioners if they are to implement a needs-led assessment in ways that are compatible with the independent living movement, while Ellis (1993) highlights the institutional and attitudinal barriers to user-participation. She argues that despite the powerless position professionals may perceive themselves as being in, they do have the discretion to choose between competing models of practice in assessment. It is they who will implement the assessment procedures of their agencies and it is they who will reinterpret them against the interests of their clients if they so choose. Good practice in assessment will involve a clear understanding of the power dynamics that operate between the social worker and disabled person for these are central to an incorporation of the social model of disability. Holdsworth goes one stage further and argues not only for a clear understanding of disability as a form of oppression, but that the principal outcome of an assessment should therefore be geared to services that are empowering:

> . . . much social work practice with disabled people is based on the individual model of disability and seeks to perpetuate

predominant societal stereotypes. However, if social workers were to change their way of working, what might be the characteristics of an empowerment model of social work with physically disabled people? Probably the most important of these, having accepted the implications of the social model of disability and the concept of disability as oppression, is the ability to start where the client is, as any individual disabled person could be at any point along a continuum of power and powerlessness and will therefore need a service geared to her specific needs for empowerment. (Holdsworth, 1991:27)

While empowerment may be central to the assessment and service provision processes, it is important that it is understood from a social-model perspective. Throughout recent years empowerment has become part of the rhetoric of central government, local authorities and the social work profession and has reached the point where it is an organising principle for institutional change in the public and private sectors (Baistow, 1995), but this does not mean that it will result in any benefit for disabled people. We discuss this in more detail in Chapter 7 but suffice to say at this point that empowerment is not something that should be thought of as the gift of social workers. Freire (1972) has argued the case that empowerment is a process in which powerless people themselves take power away from the powerful. Social workers are in a position of power as are their employing agencies and the various levels of government. If they have a role to play in the process of disabled people empowering themselves, it will be as allies and as people who are prepared to give up and share their own power.

It would not be appropriate at this point to make more detailed suggestions about how assessments should be done, but in conclusion two points need emphasis. Assessments that take account of individual and social aspects of disability and the relationship between them need to be undertaken by competent and knowledgeable professionals in collaboration with disabled people to ensure that they take into account the wishes, concerns and goals of their clients. Most importantly, if the social dimension is included, then it is social workers who need to be involved because they are concerned with the tertiary level of intervention which, when approached as an issue of empowerment, has the potential to become a primary-level intervention in terms of a social-model of disability. To finish as the chapter began, the social-model needs to be applied to both impairment and disability, otherwise the criticism levelled by Corrigan and Leonard will remain unchallenged:

> In the field of physical handicap, for example, symptomatic treatment at the individual level is still the primary response; in the case of bronchitis, structural responses would require a substantial indictment of methods of economic production; in the case of mental disorder, medical models of treatment are still dominant, a dominance which allows the neglect of structural factors in the creation of mental disorders. Poverty itself, and the stigma associated with it, is indissolubly linked in both definition and service delivery to individual pathological conceptions. (Corrigan and Leonard, 1979:101)

4

Disability in the Family

The social model of disability can be a useful and sensitising perspective in considering the implications of disability for family life. There are three ways in which the 'disability relationship' discussed in the previous chapter is important here. To begin with, the disablement of an impaired individual may be exacerbated by the way he or she is treated by the family, as with the way some disabled children are overprotected by their anxious parents. In addition, family structure and stability may be adversely affected by one of its members becoming disabled, though it is important to note that such an occurrence may strengthen rather than weaken familial ties in some situations. Finally, there is the question of the way society treats families, through social policy provision, where there is a disabled member.

These themes will be interwoven in this chapter, but to begin with it is necessary to consider the consequences of disability within the family and the scope and possibility for social work intervention. To locate the family in its appropriate social context it needs to be recognised that it is a universal social group which in one form or another occurs in all societies and at all times.

In Britain there has been a tendency to overromanticise historical aspects of family life, seeing families in the past as much more capable of looking after their own, particularly weaker, members and coping in times of stress. However, it is sometimes argued that in the past 100 years family size has reduced considerably and the past extended family has become the modern two-generation nuclear family. Also, the family has lost many of its functions to the state, which provides education for all children, care and treatment for sick members and economic support in times of unemployment.

The accuracy of this picture of family life is still the subject of much debate. Some writers have argued that the nuclear family has always been the basic family unit, while others have suggested that there is little evidence to support the notion that the family was better able and more willing to support other family members in the past than it is now. Certainly it is true that there have been a number of very important changes in the nature of the family. First, there has been a rapid increase in marital breakdown; the numbers of couples divorcing rose from 25 400 in 1961 to 155 500 in 1995 in England and Wales although most of this increase occurred in the early 1970s following the Divorce Reform Act 1969. The Family Policies Study Centre (1997) estimate that on current trends, 28 per cent of children will experience their parents divorcing before they are 16 years old. Second, and as a consequence of this, there are many more one-parent families, though some are of short-term duration because people re-marry: in 1994, remarriages accounted for 40 per cent of all marriages (Family Policies Study Centre, 1997) while the 1994 General Household Survey found that 23 per cent of households with dependent children were lone-parent families. Finally, the increasing numbers of elderly people in the population at large has placed an additional caring responsibilities on many families. By the year 2001 it is estimated that 16 per cent of the population will be over 65 years of age and at least 2 per cent will be over 85 years. This represents a 25-fold increase over the century (Family Policies Study Centre, 1997).

Young and Willmott (1973) characterised the present-day family as 'symmetrical': that is, where often both the husband and wife work but family life is centred on the home and family members share most of the domestic tasks. This is, however, to some extent an idealisation of family for in 1996 official figures put the number of people unemployed at just over 2 million while the Labour government elected in 1997 claimed that this meant that one in five households had no earned income. Furthermore, while people tend to agree that household tasks should be shared, it remains the case that in the majority of families, these fall to women. However, when a disability occurs within the family this does limit the possibility of sharing tasks and may also exacerbate other internal and external pressures on the family. As Topliss puts it:

> Although the precise impact of disablement upon family life depends upon the position within the family of the disabled person, a growing body of literature suggests that whether it is a handicapped husband, wife, child or elderly parent who is affected, disablement has an important effect on the relationship and opportunities of the family as a whole. (Topliss, 1979:129)

What is being suggested is that in considering the consequences of disability within the family, external economic and social pressures on family life need to be taken account of, as well as the impact of the disability itself upon individual members and the family as a unit. Families with an impaired member may be further disabled by poor housing, poverty, lack of emotional support and the lack of social provision generally.

Children with disabilities

The birth of a disabled child can be a traumatic and shattering event for a family, and that is the dominant way both professionals involved and researchers have treated the subject. As a consequence it has usually been assumed that as well as needing appropriate information and practical assistance, parents also need skilled help to overcome the loss, grief and bereavement they feel as a consequence of failing to produce a healthy child. This view is summarised by Selfe and Stow:

> Many writers have dealt with the initial emotions experienced by parents. These often include extreme feelings of shock, helplessness, shame, embarrassment and guilt. In addition there may well be feelings of frustration, and rejection of the child. Some psychologists have seen this as part of the process of grief and mourning for the normal child who was never born. Others conceive parents to be in a

state of chronic sorrow because they are faced with the life-long reality of their situation. (Selfe and Stow, 1981:205)

However, this view does not pass completely unchallenged, and others have suggested that the birth of a disabled child does not, of necessity, promote adverse emotional reactions (Roith, 1974; Avery, 1997), while Baldwin argues that even where stress is present it may stem from unresolved practical problems:

> Many writers, particularly those who are themselves professionals or addressing professional audiences, take as their starting point the assumption that severe disablement in a child has abnormal and pathological effects upon the family. This approach is often used to justify professional judgements about the kind of help families 'need'. It can also, as Wilkin [1979:41] argues, lead to neglect of the practical problems of day to day living. Above all, it tends to neglect the fact that disabled children are individuals, bringing their own rewards and stresses, happiness and disappointments, much the same as other children. The assumption made here is that severe disablement almost invariably creates practical problems. Providing help with these can relieve stress on families and enable them to function, as far as possible, like other families. (in Walker and Townsend, 1981:124)

Thus, in discussing the impact of a disabled child upon family life, differing views based upon the individual and social-models of disability once again emerge.

Lonsdale, who carried out her own study, makes sense of these differing views in the following way:

> It is known that some parents cope and some do not, but as yet we have little explanation of the reasons for this. It might be that there are links between being able to manage and having adequate finances, or with enjoying secure relationships within the family, or with the nature of handicap itself, or it might be a combination of all three. The nature of the problems suggest that it is an area for social work involvement but of what kind and when it is likely to be

most helpful has perhaps been insufficiently considered. (in Lonsdale *et al.*, 1979:1)

There are thus at least three areas where social work has an important role to play: in providing emotional support when needed, in providing access to practical assistance and resources, and in reducing the negative impact that dealing with an un-feeling professionalised bureaucracy may often have. These need to be considered separately.

In dealing with the emotional impact upon the family, it should be stressed that not all families will need professional help. However, for those that do, Jordan issues the following warning:

> Social workers do not 'know the right way' for people to react in such circumstances, still less should they impose their stereotyped formulae on others' suffering. Rather they are there to help people find their own way through their crises, and to provide a substitute for or complement to the fellow-feeling once given mainly by the afflicted to each other. (in Lonsdale *et al.*, 1979:viii)

Despite this warning, Lonsdale, in the first paper in this book, is stuck within the individual model of disability and makes recommendations accordingly:

> Handicap and mourning are inextricably linked. The birth of an obviously severely impaired child is often accompanied by a sound of silence followed by sotto voce discussion amongst midwives and doctors and a quick removal and separation of baby from the mother. The mother, and the father if he has been present at the delivery, know that something is wrong. Just how wrong they may have to wait to know, but from that moment a psychological process is set in motion. Parents begin a grief reaction to the loss of something they had been anticipating for nine months or longer, and that is a normal baby. Part of the aim when telling parents is to facilitate the grieving process that follows, and *the main role of the social worker is to help the parents to grieve in a healthy way*. (in Lonsdale *et al.*, 1979:5, our emphasis)

As well as neglecting the practical problems that may arise, Lonsdale is too accepting of the universality of grief processes. At least one writer has cynically suggested that ideas of grieving and mourning may be inappropriately applied to areas other than death, and have been extended largely as a consequence of the paucity of other social work theories:

> Another way of padding the depleted number of deaths in order to shore up the relevance of grief theory is the notion of helping the parents of children born with handicaps to grieve for the perfect child who isn't.
>
> When you come to think of it there isn't much else theoretical which is taught on your average social work method course except grieving and mourning. (Baird, 1980)

This is not to argue that some parents may not experience a grief reaction, but rather that social work practice should not begin with that assumption. Issues concerning assessment discussed in the previous chapter are equally important in working with families with a disabled child and the social model of disability is just as appropriate. Middleton (1992) uses this model to challenge the emphasis put on the parents' reactions to the birth and to consider what it might mean to the child. She argues that the first two of ten hurdles that disabled children have to overcome are getting born and then getting accepted. Getting born may prove difficult if an impairment is diagnosed during the mother's pregnancy, for this will almost certainly result in consideration and maybe recommendation that the child be aborted. If this hurdle is overcome, though, the question is how the child gets to be accepted by her family as something more than a disappointment and how she then develops a strong self-identity.

The skills of social workers in helping to achieve this are not necessarily different or new but they have to practice them within an understanding of the causes of disablement. If the child is seen as the problem and as deficient then it follows that the grief of the parents is natural and to be expected. If, however, the child is seen as someone who will be disabled by the social reactions towards her impairment, it would be the anger and frustration with the social barriers that would be the expected and understandable response. Emotional reactions to such births therefore appear to be the result of the way in which disability has been socially constructed. Barnes (1997) draws on anthropological evidence that children born with impairments are not seen in a negative light in all societies, to support the argument that disability is a product of the material and social forces in western culture, but even in the west there have been exceptions to this attitude. In her study of deafness in Martha's Vineyard, Groce (1985) describes how the birth of a hearing child was felt to be preferable but the birth of a deaf child was not in any way a cause for mourning or even regret.

While the need for emotional support can therefore be redirected to being a need for help in adjusting social attitudes, this may of course produce anger and frustration within parents at the way in which others in society are reacting towards their children. Just as the social worker may be called upon to help a child develop her self identity through perhaps assertiveness skills, so too may she be called upon to support the parents in a similar way. By moving from the individual to the social model, what the social worker does is to refocus her intervention on the help needed to become aware of and deal with disabling barriers.

What is also clear is that social workers must adopt a flexible approach and not base their interventions on preconceived ideas or theories of how families cope. Elfer (in Lonsdale *et al.*, 1979) describes his experiences working with families with a terminally-ill child and says that he began with two assumptions: that the child should be told about his illness, and the family encouraged to talk about it. These assumptions were soon lost when he found that help had to be geared, not to normative assumptions about a healthy family life, but to the way in which each family coped. Thus he found that there were few if any ground-rules upon which to structure his intervention and he concluded:

> Perhaps the only one is the importance of offering help quickly – but situations that occur can be so threatening, painful or bizarre that responses have to be those that seem right and appropriate for the situation, however unorthodox. (in Lonsdale *et al.*, 1979:6).

Thus in providing emotional support the appropriate place to start is with the coping strategy of the family itself, and while it is important not to see some reactions as pathological and others as healthy, to work towards ensuring that they are not disabling to the child. This means that the social worker will often be working in a situation of uncertainty, but better this than attempt to impose a professional definition upon a personal problem.

A second area in which families with a disabled child may need help is in the area of practical problems. Swain (1981), in his discussion of disability in the family, sees the main practical problems as suitable housing, a reasonable income, reduction of the limitations on mobility that may be caused, and perhaps an increase in time and energy spent on the 'normal' child-care tasks that all parents are required to undertake. He concludes:

> In general, however, families with disabled members experience changes in circumstances (including job opportunities and suitability of housing) which can lead to circumscribed resources and increased demands upon time and energy. The functioning of the family depends upon the way they organise themselves and adapt their environment in the face of such changes. (Swain, 1981:19)

Certainly it can be part of the social worker's job to help in this organising and adapting: in making sure that the family is receiving all the financial benefits it is entitled to, contacting organisations like the Family Fund where necessary, and negotiating with other agencies such as housing departments. It is also necessary however for social workers to assess and provide a range of services from their own agencies, particularly if they are working in the statutory sector.

Since its implementation, services for disabled children have been removed from other welfare enactments that apply to adults and are provided under the Children Act 1989. Although the definitions of disability remain the same, children are no longer subject to the restricted list of services that appeared in the CSDPA 1970 but can expect that:

Every local authority shall provide services designed –

(a) to minimise the effect on disabled children within their area of their disabilities; and

(b) to give such children the opportunity to lead lives which are as normal as possible.

(Children Act 1989, Schedule 2, Part 1, Section 6)

Despite its use of the term 'normal' that is indicative of the influence of the individual model of disability, this Act does open up the possibility of services that are innovative and relevant to the removal of disabling barriers. On one hand the inclusion of disabled children in this Act should ensure that they are not treated differently to other children, but there are difficulties in that social services do not deal with all children and this affects their concept of normal. Often this results in placing the responsibility for disability services in teams that are primarily concerned with child protection and it inevitably means the marginalisation of the former. Middleton (1995) suggests that this has been made worse by the separate Department of Health guidance on working with disabled children under this Act, which has allowed disinterested social workers to remain detached. Both managers and practitioners need to ensure that the statutory responsibilities towards disabled children are taken seriously if they are to contribute to the removal of disabling barriers. The marginalisation of such services is oppressive and part of the process of disabling children which the Children Act seeks to minimise.

A final area where families may need help is in dealing with the stresses created by their dealings with apparently unfeeling professionals and bureaucracies. There is much evidence that doctors are particularly poor at telling parents about their disabled child, as Ballard (in Lonsdale *et al.*, 1979) vividly shows in discussing his own experience, while the Collins family (in Brechin *et al.*, 1981) graphically describe the way they were shunted from one place and professional to another with little or no help offered. Robinson (1978), in his discussion of the relationship between professionals and clients with a disabled child, encapsulates his findings in the title of his book *In Worlds Apart*. He identifies a number of dimensions of the problem, including poor communication between the doctor and parents and the failure of professionals to acknowledge, let alone deal with, parental feelings of discomfort or threat. In addition he found that parents felt powerless with regard to decisions made about their child's future and some professionals individually behaved in an autocratic way. Finally, the service offered was of itself inadequate.

Again social workers can be involved in two important ways: first, as members of teams involved in telling parents, they can try to ensure that it is done in the most appropriate and humane way possible; and, second, they can provide emotional support for parents who may need to resolve their feelings of anger and distress about the way they have been treated.

In this section on families with a disabled child, the fact that most space has been devoted to emotional reactions of the families concerned does not mean that this is regarded as the most important problem. Rather, it is the problem to which social work has devoted most attention and it is for this reason that it has been considered at length. However, the need for practical assistance may in many cases be paramount and social work assistance with locating and providing appropriate resources may be crucial. This once again suggests a shift in focus, away from the individual model and towards a social-model of disability.

Abuse of disabled children

Disabled children have remained largely hidden in respect of child abuse and the response of social work despite the growth of interest and awareness in the past 20 years as to how this affects other non-disabled children. An indication of their absence in the literature and practice of child protection is that even within the first edition of this book there was no section related to what is generally considered one of the most controversial and demanding roles of social work. In the last decade, however, a few writers (Brown and Craft, 1989; Kennedy, 1989; Kelly, 1992; Marchant and Page, 1992; Middleton, 1992, 1995; Westcott, 1993; Westcott and Cross, 1995; Morris, 1997b) have begun to discuss the issue and to identify a range of ways in which disabled children are abused.

Child protection practice recognises four main forms of abuse: neglect, physical, sexual and emotional. All of these can happen to disabled children as much as any other child, if not more, but they may occur for different reasons in some circumstances and there are some additional forms of abuse that may be specific to them. The main issues of abuse of disabled children are threefold: first, that child protection services have ignored their abuse. This happens because they fail to acknowledge that it could happen, or because services that are geared to families miss the abuse that occurs in residential school settings, or because abusive acts towards disabled children are treated as a normal and tolerable reaction of overstressed parents, or because social workers lack the appropriate communication skills. Second, the institutionalisation of disabled children by the education system in particular leaves them not only vulnerable to abuse by non-family members, but it also denies them a role in mainstream society that other children enjoy. Finally, the imposition of a non-disabled normality through activities such as conductive education can act as a form of identity abuse. While there is insufficient space here to consider the practice of child protection *per se*, the purpose of this section is to highlight the most pertinent issues that affect disabled children and to consider what the social model might mean in terms of the response of social work, the police and courts which tend to see such abuse as unbelievable or the fantasy of disabled children.

The absence of disabled children within child protection services is obviously a major cause of concern, precisely because it appears not to be of concern to those services. Middleton reports that in the volumes of research that were commissioned by the Department of Health following the Cleveland enquiry into child abuse, there is only 'one passing reference to disabled children as special victims which relates to the special problems facing some parents'. She goes on to explain that this research

conceptualises child abuse as socially constructed, reflecting the values of society. If this is essentially true, it follows that the official failure to deal with the abuse of disabled children reflects a cultural lack of concern for their welfare. Disabled children will only be better protected when we learn as a society to value them equally. (Middleton, 1995:70)

There is no doubt that disabled children are abused (Westcott, 1993; Westcott and Cross, 1995) despite the official denial of the problem. Understanding why this is the case is key to changing the situation, both in terms of reducing the level of abuse and in terms of getting the child protection services to act. Middleton (1995) suggests that the situation arises from a combination of factors, and while these interact in a complex manner it is worth separating them in order to consider how they have failed disabled children:

- It is paradoxical that non-disabled adults who operate the protection services find it difficult to believe that the children they see only as vulnerable could ever be the target of an abuser, despite the evidence that abusers prey on vulnerability. This reflects the social norm of viewing disability as a personal tragedy and seeing disabled people only in terms of the help and assistance they need, rather than as having the same potential as non-disabled people, even when that potential may be greater.
- Social workers, as representatives of the welfare system, may consider that much of the abuse that disabled children suffer is acceptable. The dominant ideology that sees the disabled child as a burden on an otherwise happy family is forgiving of lapses in the patience of parents. While this certainly arises from the failure to see disabled people as anything more than dependent and as the cause of the problem, it also reflects some collusion on the part of social workers and their agencies in their failure to provide adequate support to families with disabled children. Furthermore, this acceptance is not limited to disabled children and occurs, for example, when abuse is considered a natural response to poverty.
- Some abuse may not be recognised as such because it does not happen to non-disabled children. Rough handling of

children requiring personal assistance, or the failure to ensure that certain aids and equipment are changed as the child grows or are fitted carefully are common. This is reframed in terms of the treatment of the child rather than as a form of abuse and reflects the strength of the process of medicalising disability that is integral to the individual model.

- For some disabled children, the problem arises because the child protection services generally have no means of communicating other than with non-disabled children. This is both in terms of the general lack of communication skills such as sign language, but also due to the tendency to understand the world, including abuse, in terms of a non-disabled culture. Throughout the welfare system and society at large, the issue of communication is seen as a problem of the individual who cannot talk or hear, rather than as society's failure to be inclusive of other communication systems. This results in disabled children being unable to give evidence or even being heard.

- Finally, abuse may be considered as an acceptable price to pay for otherwise resolving an administratively difficult problem. Many children, for example, are sent to residential schools or may be placed with foster families in which they are subsequently abused. These resources may be quite scarce because of the reluctance of other foster parents or of mainstream schools to accommodate disabled children, so the additional problem to the social services authority of placing the child if she were to be removed outweighs the abuse. Whilst this may be the least worst option from an administrative-model perspective, it is not, in the language of child care, in the best interests of the child.

While these reactions to impairment in children may be explicable through the analysis of the social model of disability, they also illustrate the depth of the influence of the individual model within social work. The institutional structures of social services agencies in which disability is seen as separate from other child care services and particularly child protection, and the cultural beliefs of social workers that have created a number of myths that either disabled children are not abused or that what might constitute abuse with a non-disabled child should be understood as a natural reaction of parents to the stress the child causes, both tend to mitigate against an approach that treats disabled children appropriately. The problem, however, is not simply one of an inadequate response, but also possibly one of collusion.

Morris (1997b), in a review of literature on the placement of disabled children in boarding schools and care homes, found that social services departments may be using such placements as a means of avoiding intervening in child care issues and this may include cases of abuse to disabled children. This not only reflects discrimination against individual children, but on an institutional level it is qualitatively different to the response they would have had if the child was not disabled. These problems are not resolved by simple policy changes, although they are important, and ideas such as replacing child-protection conferences with children-in-need conferences might go some way to breaking down the organisational barriers. What is also required is for the culture of understanding to be changed. This can only be achieved by challenging the assumptions on which it is based and which have been internalised by many social workers and agencies, or they will continue to curtail those who seek to practice appropriately.

Middleton (1995) argues that social workers must respond to the challenge of child abuse as part of an anti-oppressive practice that leads to a breakdown of artificial institutional boundaries and that doesn't seek to polarise the interests of the child and her parents on the basis of one being the victim of the others who are totally bad. However, child protection services are facing their own political and practice problems that often mitigate against the inclusion of disability issues. The other components of an anti-oppressive strategy therefore would need to include awareness-raising and an understanding of the nature of disablement. These are training issues that will be discussed further in Chapter 7, but two factors should be stressed. First, social work practice will not progress unless it is modified to incorporate the social model of disability. This is not simply an academic debate, for what we see in examining child abuse is that it is the individual model of disability that causes the child protection services to ignore disabled children. Second, it is insufficient to simply direct training at those specialists who express an interest. The lesson of child protection's failure to protect disabled children is that any disability awareness training must include the majority of social workers and their managers, while recognising that the role of specialists is complex and must not be sacrificed.

The issue of abuse of disabled children also needs to consider the cultural and structural barriers that exclude them or try to control and limit their self-identity as disabled people. Finkelstein and Stuart (1996), for example, seek an ending of the treatment of disabled children as children with 'special needs', arguing that this arises out of a cultural belief that their lives have a lesser value than those of non-disabled children. The changes they seek start at conception with an end to screening programmes. They argue that the impairment of a foetus places no additional risk on the mother during pregnancy or at birth, and that the future quality of life of the child is not a ground for abortion. They highlight instead the need for family support and the right of the child not to be over-protected on some false assumption of their inability to take responsibility for themselves, as well as the ending of segregated education. Morris (1997b) also identifies the lack of family support as a factor in causing a correlation between severity of impairment and the likelihood of residential care being considered an option by social services. However, being put into care as a disabled child not only means a segregated childhood, but it will often continue on into residential care as an adult. Not only do placements in residential homes lead to an increased risk of recognised forms of abuse, it is a level of deprivation that is not experienced by non-disabled people.

The final area is concerned with emotional abuse and the denial of self-identity. The issue mentioned earlier in this respect was that of conductive education, which remains the subject of considerable debate (Beardshaw, 1993; Oliver, 1993), but nevertheless serves as a good example of what this might mean. In a society that is dominated by the individual model in which normality is seen as the lack of any impairment, it is difficult for anyone who deviates from this norm to develop a positive self-identity, as they are treated as abnormal. Yet this has been identified as an important element of the struggle of disabled people to remove the barriers that confront them. This is quite different from overcoming difficulties in the functional sense. The development of a positive self-identity is necessary to individuals seeking to assert their own value and citizenship alongside others. What is problematic about conductive education is that it aims to train people to conform to a non-disabled normality and in the process devalues diversity. This is also the case when deaf children are prevented from learning sign language by being sent to special schools that only allow lip reading; they are being denied the right to become part of a linguistic culture and expected to conform to the hearing norm. Morris describes the importance of pride to disabled people:

> When a mother says that she loves her child 'in spite' of that child's disability, she is saying that she does not love the disabled part of her child. When the Spastics Society urges the public to 'see the person and not the wheelchair', they are being asked to ignore something that is central to our experience. And when our achievements are applauded as 'overcoming all odds', the disabled part of us is being denied and diminished.
>
> Valuing us as people should not mean ignoring the things about our bodies which make us different. In asserting our rights we also want to take pride in ourselves. We cannot do this unless this pride incorporates the way we are different. (Morris, 1992:6)

Childhood is a formative period of life and the impact both then and later in adulthood of having one's life devalued can be enormous. Emotional abuse is not usually considered as important as the others – physical, sexual and neglect – but the potential for it to occur within a society that devalues impairment is high so it is a matter that should underpin social work with disabled children, both within child protection and elsewhere.

Growing up with a disability: making relationships

Certainly many disabled young people experience difficulties in making relationships of either a social or a sexual nature, and there are a number of factors in this, some of which may be related to individual problems and others which may be a consequence of the social and physical environment. Stewart sums this up when he says that:

> Disabled people sometimes have severe relationship diffi-culties, either through sheer lack of opportunity for meet-ing and involvement with other people, or through deficiency in the emotional and social skills which enable adequate development and maintenance of friendships and love af-fairs. (Stewart, 1979:20–1)

However, there is a problem with the assumption that the lack of opportunities and deficiency in skills are two separate issues, as the former will certainly lead to the latter. In other words, it is the experience of special schools and overprotec-tion during childhood that fails to equip people with the ability to develop relationships alongside their peers rather than the presence of an impairment. Furthermore, the reactions of non-disabled people who have themselves had an education away from disabled children are unlikely to ease the process. Spe-cific aspects of these problems need to be discussed in a little more detail in order to clarify areas where social work inter-vention may be appropriate.

Disabled people may not have the same opportunity for meeting other people. Many social gatherings such as youth clubs and discos may simply be physically inaccessible, and in a wheelchair it may not always be possible to participate in that favourite teenage pastime of hanging around on street corners. Disabled people may also find it difficult to initiate contacts in pubs or at parties. To take the initiative and take a seat close to someone who is attractive may be very difficult for someone in a wheelchair, and for visually impaired people it may be impossible. Parents of disabled youngsters are some-times overprotective and reluctant to allow their children to take the usual teenage risks. Furthermore, disabled teenagers may also find it difficult to do things that perhaps they should not (when they go out they probably have to be transported by their parents). They therefore can't lie to their parents about where they have been or who they have been with.

Special schools are often criticised for exacerbating these problems in a number of ways. For a start they usually take disabled youngsters away from their own home environment and peers for most of the year, and by the time they eventually leave these segregated establishments peer relationships have often been formed in their local community on a lasting basis and they find themselves excluded. Criticism is often levelled at these schools not only in terms of the educational standards they provide, but also because they fail to provide remedial social skills programmes to alleviate the negative effects of segregation. Hence special education may further disable impaired adolescents and offer nothing 'special'. These criticisms are very serious when it is borne in mind that there has been little change in the proportion of disabled children who are still educated in special schools. Barnes (1991) examined the educational statistics from the Department for Education and Science which showed that between 1977, the year of the Warnock Report, and 1989, the proportion of school children in special schools had fallen by only 0.06 per cent, from 1.41 to 1.35 per cent. Furthermore, he argues that in itself this figure is misleading as many local authorities have in fact increased their segregated education over this period, a few by as much as 25 per cent.

Another major problem for disabled people in making and sustaining relationships is the reaction of other people. There are two aspects of this. Other people may be prejudiced towards the disabled individual or indeed may simply be uncertain about how to treat him or her – should the disability be ignored or spoken about openly, and, if the latter, at what stage in the relationship should such questions be raised? Such uncertainty is a product of the lack of contact caused by segregated education. On the other hand, disabled people may be unsure or simply lack experience about how to present themselves to other people. This may occur as a consequence of over-protection by parents, or again through segregation during their education. Thus disabled people may be too intense in their personal relationships or may want to move to different stages in a given relationship too quickly. It is certainly clear that other people are a part of the problem, for, as American sociologist Edwin Lemert has commented:

Although physical handicaps partially restrict opportunities for achievement, the more critically operating limits come from an overlay of interpersonal and formal social barriers founded upon cultural stereotypes about physical defects. As many physically disadvantaged people say, the problem is less the handicap than it is the people. (Lemert, 1967:16–17)

Stewart shows how making relationships for disabled people may be more of a problem for disabled young people than for others:

Our relationships, including our sexual relationships, are formed mainly within our circle of established acquaintances, and the smaller the circle, the less the opportunity. The part which unsuitable ingress to premises plays in limiting social – and hence relationship – activities for handicapped people is incalculable. Admittedly, some disabled people will make use of this excuse to withdraw from social life, but for others it remains the main problem. (Stewart, 1979:36)

So the main problems involved in making relationships with disabled youngsters are the physical environment, the response of others, segregative educational practices, over-protection and the lack of experience that some disabled people themselves have in coping with the demands of an able-bodied world. Sensitive social work intervention should take account of the possible presence of some of these factors and should encourage disabled youngsters to take their place in the world and not be segregated from it in schools, day centres and residential units.

On an organisational level the problem has been identified as one of transition between different services; that is, between the education services which provide support for disabled children and adolescents, and social services which provide services for disabled adults. The Disabled Persons (Services, Consultation and Representation) Act 1986 specifically addressed this issue in sections 5 and 6 which lay down a framework for these two agencies to communicate with each other in order to ensure the transfer of responsibility and a smooth transition for disabled adolescents.

However, as the Social Services Inspectorate (1995, 1997) project into this issue has shown, it requires more than administrative procedures. These reports also place an emphasis on the need for interrelated policy-making between children's and adult services, for the inclusion of disabled youngsters in that policy-making process, for the development of social-work skills in working with families with disabled children, and for the use of disability-equality training as a means of promoting the social model of disability.

Furthermore, they recognise the need to go beyond the two agencies that are by statute required to communicate and to involve GPs, health authorities, housing departments and employers in the process. Each of these contribute to the production of a disabling environment and therefore need to make changes to their own practices if disabled children are to be enabled to enter adult life with the opportunities available to non-disabled people.

Sex and disability

The attention paid to sex and disabled people has tended to focus on problems, and the manner in which subsequent interventions have occurred have often been 'unhelpful because they are mechanistic, depoliticised, and outdated' (Shakespeare, 1997:183). In fact, it could be argued that this aspect of disabled people's lives has received too much attention and that it should be returned to where it belongs – to people's private lives. Certainly it is true to say that the attention attracted by the 'sex and disability industry' reveals as much about society's own values as it does about the sexual aspects of the lives of disabled people. Once again, then, the individual and social models of disability need to be considered in relation to sex – the individual sexual problems that some disabled people may have (individual model), and value-judgements concerning appropriate and acceptable ways of expressing sexuality in present-day society (social model).

Stewart provided some of the earlier material on the sexual problems of individual disabled people. In his own survey he found:

Over half the disabled people interviewed (searchingly and at some length) were found to be subject to current, personal, significant sexual problems: the precise proportion was 54%. A further 18% had experienced such problems since the onset of their disorders (whether at birth or later) but these had become less significant – having been solved by personal effort, infrequently resolved by suitable advice or counsel, all too often fading into insignificance only with time and custom. (Stewart, 1979:39)

There is little other empirical evidence about whether the proportion of disabled people experiencing sexual difficulties is greater than the rest of the population or not, though Morris (1989) does add a more qualitative dimension to the meaning of that experience for women with spinal injuries, and more recently Shakespeare *et al.* (1996) have contributed significantly to the literature with their biographical and analytical account of sexuality focusing on gay and lesbian relationships. Stewart's findings also need to be qualified by the fact that the numbers in his sample were fairly small, and as a sexual counsellor it is likely that he would be sensitive to this particular aspect of disabled people's lives. Certainly the assumption made by some professionals that sexual relations are an inevitable problem for disabled people and their partners is unwarranted.

The relevance of this discussion for social work intervention is that it would be wrong to assume that all disabled people have unresolved sexual problems of one kind or another, but that when it is apparent that there are sexual problems it might be useful to have some understanding of possible causes. Pain or lack of sensation may be factors which make it difficult to achieve satisfactory sexual fulfilment for both parties, as may impotence, depending upon the particular medical condition. Real or imagined physical danger can also affect sexual performance, as can the side-effects of some medication. Incontinence and incontinence devices may also inhibit or affect sexual relations. Finally, it has been clearly established that psychological factors like fear, anxiety and a poor self-image can also adversely affect sexual performance.

It would be foolish to deny that most disabled people are

impaired in sexual performance if we take the dominant cultural values of completed coitus and multiple orgasms as the standard. However, that does not imply that it is not possible for the vast majority of disabled people to achieve satisfactory sexual relations. The problem then may be one of social expectations and cultural values rather than impaired individual performance, though of course the discrepancy between social expectations and individual performance may be experienced as personal inadequacy. Shakespeare explains how these expectations operate:

> In the realm of sex and love, the generalised assumption that disability is a medical tragedy becomes dominant and inescapable. In modern western societies, sexual agency is considered the essential element of full adult personhood, replacing the role formerly taken by paid work: because disabled people are infantalised, and denied the status of active subjects, consequently their sexuality is undermined. This also works the other way, in that the assumption of asexuality is a contributing factor towards the disregard of disabled people. (Shakespeare, 1996:192)

The social model of disability may also throw light on the sexual problems of disabled people in day-centres and residential establishments, in that often these problems are in the minds of professionals rather than disabled people themselves. They stem from decisions made about segregating disabled people in particular kinds of institutions and the rules made in them to regulate all behaviour, including sexual. That is not to deny that there are genuine moral dilemmas to be resolved concerning issues like helping disabled people to masturbate if they are unable to do it themselves, or putting them in a bed of their choice and not where staff think they should be. These issues are not only related to sex, however, but also to things like smoking cannabis and many other activities. The point is that problems created by non-disabled people organising services in particular ways are often turned around and located at the level of individual disabled people. The practice of social work within a social model would require an end to this process of pathologising, and the development of an awareness of the support that individuals might need when faced with such barriers. Furthermore, it requires individual social workers to examine their own prejudices which may contribute to the negative stereotypes which see the sexuality of disabled people, whether heterosexual or homosexual, as perverted and limited to relationships with other disabled people.

Disability, marriage and partnership

Sex may or may not be a problem in long-term relationships where one or both of the partners are disabled. But certainly there may also be practical problems of housing or mobility, and most of the aids and adaptations are geared to the single person: ripple mattresses are not made in double sizes and extensions to houses are usually only built to accommodate the disabled person, regardless of whether there is a partner or not. Even with new housing, the provision of wheelchair accessibility and mobility in dwellings in the rented social housing sector is disproportionately skewed towards single-person accommodation, not only causing a practical problem to many people but reflecting the dominance of a social attitude in which disabled people are not seen as being part of a family or other relationship.

However, what little evidence there is on the break up of marriages where there is a disabled member is conflicting. Topliss (1979) in a survey in Southampton found that 16 per cent of disabled women were divorced or separated compared with a national divorce rate of 7 per cent at the time. However, only 4 per cent of disabled men were divorced. Sainsbury (1970) suggests that marriages are more likely to break up when the wife rather than the husband is disabled. On the other hand, Blaxter (1980) in her study in Scotland found that the divorce rate among disabled men exceeded that among disabled women. In Morris's (1989) study of women with spinal injuries, which may not necessarily be representative of other disabled people, 17 out of 102 who were married at the time of their injury had subsequently divorced (over varying time spans), and while some account for this by individual reactions to their impairment, social expectations also played a role:

> Samantha blames her divorce partly on her consultant who told her husband that '75 per cent of marriages go bang and to get rid of the double bed. I am sure this stayed with him and did not give our personal life a chance. He left 15 months after I came home.' (Morris, 1989:83)

Again, social work intervention should not proceed on the assumption that impairments may create relationship problems; even where such problems are present they may stem from outside rather than from individual defects and hence form another aspect of the process of disablement. One way of highlighting possible stresses brought about by social expectations is through the concept of 'role'. When sociologists talk about roles, they usually mean 'behaviour oriented to the patterned expectations of others' (Merton, 1957). This then provides the link between the individual and social structure and suggests that people's behaviour takes account of social expectations, and failure to behave, or to be able to behave, in this way may create stress and conflict.

In particular, this expectation is often applied to gender, and in the past has suggested that where the man is impaired he may not be able to behave in the roles expected of him in the sphere of work, and hence his economic role may be affected. On the other hand, the social expectations of a woman have been seen as different and the presence of an impairment may be thought to have less effect upon her role performance. Today this makes inappropriate assumptions about role performances based on gender but does recognise the historical reality of dominant social expectations, as illustrated by Blaxter:

> In only a few cases did a wife's disablement cause a complete change in the family's way of life, however (when, for instance, the husband had to give up his work to care for her); for the most part the wife 'managed', with varying degrees of hardship, with formal or informal help of other women. A husband's disablement, on the other hand, meant a radical change; he might have to stay at home and adjust

to 'idleness', or change his job or conditions of work, which affected the whole family pattern. (Blaxter, 1980:203–4)

People do not, however perform roles simply based on external social expectations, and these expectations are both socially constructed and subject to change. Each individual relationship may produce its own internal expectations about the roles for each partner, and these will reflect contemporary lifestyles. It is important, therefore, for social workers to be aware of the range of role expectations on individuals, to avoid stereotyping people themselves and to be conscious of the impact of disability from the perspective of the way people may see themselves.

Disability in relationships may thus give rise to three kinds of problems: individual problems of a personal or sexual nature, problems related to lack of resources or practical provisions, and, linking the two, discrepancies between individual behaviour and social expectations. Social work assessments will need to take account of the possibility of any or all of these factors being present in order to avoid the situation described by Blaxter (1980:219) where 'Social work support for emotional and family problems tended to be available only after a crisis situation had developed, when help might be too late.' But again social workers should avoid assumptions that any or all of these problems must be present. In many relationships where there is a disability no help may be needed at all. Shearer quotes one description of what is an entirely 'normal' marriage:

My wife goes about her daily chores. I earn the living; we have friends who accept us; our bungalow is indistinguishable from the neighbouring bungalows except that possibly ours is a little better kept. My wife helps me to dress; I help her to bath; we have sexual intercourse frequently; we row about my driving; she never has enough housekeeping money; she always lacks something to wear for the special occasion; in fact, it's all very normal. (Shearer, 1981a:29–30)

Growing old with a disability

Any consideration of disability has to take into account that, by adopting a functional definition, the majority of disabled people are in fact old. It is not the intention to deal separately with the topic of social work with elderly people, for this has been covered by a number of other writers (for example, Rowlings, 1981; Scrutton, 1989; Froggatt, 1990; Hughes, 1995; Marshall, 1996; and Marshall and Dixon, 1996) and as the principle responsibilities of social services towards older people arises through their disablement, this literature tends to deal with the issue of impairments that come with ageing. Rather, it is ageing with a disability that needs to be considered.

Until recently there was virtually nothing known about the effects of growing old on disabled people, mainly because in the past few people with impairments would have survived into old age. However, the numbers who now do so have increased and some researchers (for example Morris, 1989; Zarb, 1991, 1993; Zarb *et al.*, 1990) have begun to examine the issues and the consequences for the provision of supportive environments. Zarb (1993) argues that it is important to have a conceptual framework for understanding this issue as traditional psychological concepts of ageing and policy analyses tend to be inadequate to explain the personal, physical and social consequences of ageing with a disability.

Once again the concept of career is used as it is capable of taking into account the different experiences and resources that individuals may bring with them to a similar process, and thus it helps to explain the variations in the way ageing will be experienced. However, while each individual will experience ageing differently, there are certain commonalities in terms of both individual problems associated with impairment and social problems that result from the way society has responded to this phase in the careers of disabled people. Zarb describes some of the individual issues:

> First, many people's experiences are consistent with the notion of 'premature' physical ageing; for them, ageing is characterised by a process of 'general deterioration' which appears to be more closely associated with the length of time since the onset of the impairment than with age itself. Typically there is a noticeable 'downturn' in physical well-being and health status around 20 to 30 years from onset, regardless of chronological age.

Second, many of the physical changes that people experience are perceived as being long-term effects of their
original impairments. For some groups, there are also
common secondary impairments caused either by the original
impairment, or the long-term effects of medical treatment
or rehabilitation. The most common of these is the high
incidence of arthritic and rheumatic problems; other specific
examples include blindness and neurological problems associated with long-term diabetes; chronic pain resulting from
building up immunity to certain drugs, such as morphine
(various groups); chronic respiratory problems caused by
spinal deformity (scoliosis); and a variety of physiological
problems coming under the heading of 'post-polio syndrome'.
(Zarb, 1993:190)

It is clear, therefore, that as a result of ageing individual
impairments may be exacerbated and as a consequence the
need for personal assistance will increase. However, current
social policy tends to assume the opposite because it reflects
the role expectations of society which are themselves artifi-
cially linked to chronological age. In this way the spending
limits of social service authorities on community care, which
are set relative to residential and nursing home payments,
are considerably lower for people over retirement age than
for those of working age, while direct payments may not begin
if the person is over 65 years. Similarly, social security payments are usually reduced at retirement age and some such
as the Mobility Allowance disappear altogether causing a real
drop in income to people who may have had very restricted
opportunities to earn personal pensions in the same way as
the non-disabled population.

The difficulties of ageing can be emotional as well as physical. Becoming older often causes people to reflect more on
their earlier lives, and for some disabled people such reflections may amount to a reminiscence of unfulfilled potentials.
MacFarlane (1994) argues that for disabled women in particular
this may be a time when they recall a lifetime of being deprived of the right to enjoy fulfilling relationships, of being
aware of one's own sexuality and of experiencing childbirth
and that this can prove to be a daunting task. Furthermore,

while this is itself a result of the social responses to impairment over a lifetime, she suggests it can be compounded by the policy and institutional reactions to age:

> It is agonising to look forward to the struggle of reaching the age of sixty and to know that hard fought for services and other provision will be reassessed and probably changed because of the ageing process. (MacFarlane, 1994:255).

Ageing therefore may be experienced as a time of threat, not simply from the difficulties caused by deteriorating health or emotional distress, but by the reactions of welfare agencies, in particular their readiness to view residential care as a more appropriate response to the need for personal assistance. Zarb suggests that this threat to lifestyle may be so great as to cause some people to consider euthanasia or suicide which is a terrible indictment of the role that social services play in providing 'care' to disabled people as they grow older. Clearly, then, the task for social workers as agents of such authorities must be to assist individuals to access the services that will permit them to maintain independence and choice within their own lives. Once again it is necessary to have an awareness of the individual problems that disabled people face, but it is more important to understand how these become barriers when policy responses follow an individual model of disability.

Disability and caring

One of the consequences of inadequate social services support, whether it is as a result of insufficient funding, oppressive policies or poor social work, is that it will cause disabled people of all ages to be dependent on family and friends for personal assistance. It can of course be argued that rather than viewing the lack of such services as the cause of dependent relationships, their provision at whatever level should be seen as a contribution towards reducing the dependency that results from the presence of an impairment. This, however, does not stand up to the scrutiny of comparison with many other services that are collectively provided to ensure the comfort, security and mobility of the non-disabled population; for example utilities such as water and fuel supplies, or services such as road maintenance or snow clearance. While disabled people also benefit from such services, the efficiency with which they are provided to a level that affords non-disabled people the opportunity to enjoy a satisfying lifestyle is in contrast to the social commitment to services that would allow disabled people to live independently (Finkelstein and Stuart, 1996).

In recent years, those who provide the assistance within dependent relationships have received official recognition and succeeded in having their own needs considered deserving of welfare support through the Carers (Recognition and Services) Act 1995. The early case for this was made by a combination of arguments: that carers save the state a considerable sum of money (Nissel and Bonnerjea, 1982); that the task of caring falls disproportionately on women (Equal Opportunities Commission, 1982); and through highlighting the consequences of lack of support to families which take on the role:

> An important finding is that, once the elderly person has moved in, caring is no longer seen as a shared activity. Siblings disappear, children give (and are not usually expected to) no help and the neighbourhood offers nothing. Biological ties are superseded by perceptions of women's work by the husband, as he offers no more help when his parents are involved than when his wife's parents are the dependants. Teenage children don't bring friends home; husbands disappear to work and the pub. A picture of isolation and family breakdown comes into focus. (Oliver, J., 1982:477)

There is no denying that a great deal of stress can arise from being on either side of this dependency relationship, but what is problematic are solutions that do not accord with the aims of independent living for disabled people. The recognition of carers is itself part of the problem because it reinforces the helper–helped relationship that lies at the heart of the creation of dependency by seeing their needs as relative to the 'burden' caused by the disabled person. As a result, the solutions that have been advocated, in particular by feminists seeking to reduce the exploitation of women (Finch, 1984) and which have been maintained by welfare services, have been to offer respite to carers by providing short and long-term residential care to disabled people. Such solutions that focus on the support of carers within the current policy context clearly reinforce the exclusion of disabled people from full citizenship.

Others, however (for example Croft, 1986; Morris, 1991), have argued that the interests of disabled people and women carers can be viewed as compatible if a social-model analysis is applied to the issues. In this way, what is recognised is not so much the burden on one side of the relationship, that is the carers, but that the aims of independent living are for disabled people to be free of the dependency it creates. The policy solution therefore lies in collective approaches that are based on the inclusion, not the exclusion, of disabled people from mainstream social organisation: in other words the removal of disabling barriers.

At the level of the individual and families which is where social workers are likely to be working, the creation of carers as a recognised, though unpaid, occupation is also problematic because it ignores the reality of how people live:

> Rather than assuming that the presence of a non-disabled family member creates a relationship of carer and cared-for, it is the relationship between partners, parent and child, siblings, etc. which should be recognised. Some relationships can sustain the giving of personal assistance, some cannot. Some people can facilitate independence for their partner, parent or child, some cannot. Some relationships are abusive and exploitative, some are liberating. To categorise people as carers and dependants is to gloss over all of this. (Morris, 1993:40)

This assumption of dependency can have profound effects on families, particularly through the tendency to see caring by a child for a parent as a form of role reversal. Keith and Morris (1995) argue that the construction of child carers within an individual-model analysis in which the provision of personal assistance determines dependency within a relationship, has the effect of denying the ability of disabled people to parent. Research in this area, they argue, has tended to assume that the presence of an impairment is the cause of the need to care rather than inadequate community support services. The demand therefore for more support on the basis of carer's needs is to both ignore the reality of the situation and to attribute blame to disabled people.

While the social-model perspective of this debate has gained some recognition, its full implications have yet to be appreciated by the carers' lobby. In a review of research in this area by the director of Carers National Association (Pitkeathley, 1996) the emphasis remains clearly on the needs of carers rather than establishing the rights of disabled people to be free of these dependency relationships, and, indeed, Aldridge and Becker (1996) argue that unpalatable though it may be, this approach is necessary given the economic and political realities of a residual welfare system. However, what such arguments do is to reinforce the injustice of the individual model of disability with its acceptance that disability is a welfare, not a civil rights issue.

Clearly some of these issues are beyond the ability of individual social workers to resolve, but their contribution to the administration of welfare can have a determining impact on individuals and families. The message for social workers in relation to the issue of carers is the same as it has been throughout this chapter, that is not to make assumptions about how different individuals might respond to similar situations but to work with people from their own perception of the reality of their lives. Working within families is a privilege which requires sensitivity and open-mindedness rather than a professional judgmentalism based upon politically-normative views of complex relationships.

5

Living with Disabilities

In the previous chapter, one of the main difficulties that disabled people faced at all ages was how to maintain relationships with their families while also achieving a level of independence and autonomy within them. Leat (1988) suggests that the pressures of dependency within families is the most significant cause of disabled people having to enter residential care, though this analysis was part of the Wagner report into residential care which was concerned to promote its positive use but failed to consider the impact of poor community services on these relationships. This impact may also account for the fact that disabled adults are far more likely than non-disabled people to be living alone. In 1986, 30 per cent of disabled adults were living alone (Martin *et al.*, 1989) which compares with just 11 per cent of the whole population at the time of the 1991 census. As would be expected, the proportion rises with age but even if only those under 65 years are considered, some 16 per cent of disabled adults are still living alone. This has significant implications for the provision of both housing and personal assistance which would enable these individuals to live independently, but also for the provision of support to those within families. This chapter considers the living options for younger disabled people, generally taken to mean under 65 years, and therefore discusses the issues of residential and nursing homes, day-centres, accessible housing and personal assistance.

Residential care

It has been suggested that while independent living is the preferred option for most people, it has often been the case

that the only option available to the disabled person is residential care:

> In Great Britain we have a habit of providing for 'difficult'
> minority groups in segregated institutions and those suffer-
> ing traumatic tetraplegia are no exception. It is a tradition
> which has roots in the Poor Law and which comes down to
> us today virtually unchanged. Only rarely can someone who
> depends heavily on others for personal help, and who for
> some reason does not have the support of – or wishes to
> live independently of – his or her family, find an alterna-
> tive system of accommodation and care. (Davis, in Brechin
> *et al.*, 1981:322)

While methodological differences between overall estimates
of disabled people and the occupancy of residential and nursing
homes make it difficult to directly compare the data, it is clear
that less than 5 per cent of younger disabled people with
physical or sensory impairments are living in this type of accommodation. However, according to the Personal Social Services Current Expenditure 1994–95, more than 20 per cent
of gross expenditure for this group was spent on it. Table 5.1
shows that in 1996 there were 9900 such people living in
residential and nursing homes in England. In addition, by
1986 there were 72 Young Disabled Units (YDUs) provided
by health authorities which housed an unspecified number of
disabled people (Leat, 1988).

In addition to this, it should be recognised that a significant proportion of people with learning difficulties of whom
34 900 were in residential and nursing homes, and of the
317 800 elderly people in such accommodation, will also have
physical impairments. It is clear from the OPCS disability studies
that the proportion of disabled people living in institutions
rises with age, and this was reflected in the previous chapter
through the fears of some disabled people when growing older.
While there has been little research concerning younger disabled adults in residential care, if the circumstances of their
admission are in any way similar to those of older people,
these fears may well be justified. Booth concluded from a comprehensive review of studies about elderly residents that:

Table 5.1 *Numbers of adult residents in residential and nursing homes in England, 1996.*

	All residential, nursing and small homes	Local authority residential homes	Registered residential homes		Registered nursing homes	Registered small homes	
			Voluntary	Private		Voluntary	Private
All client groups	428 120	64 200	60 300	167 720	123 600	1 700	10 600
Eldery people	317 800	50 800	35 600	140 200	87 100	100	4 000
Physical/sensorily disabled adults	9 900	1 100	5 200	1 100	2 200	100	200
Elderly mentally infirm people	26 800	2 500	1 100	6 800	16 400		
People with mental illness	16 700	1 500	3 900	6 400	3 000	200	1 700
People with learning disabilities	34 900	200	13 600	12 700	2 700	1 200	4 500
Other/unknown	3 570	90	1 500	520	12 300	30	200

Source: Department of Health (1996).

Most people do not themselves make a positive choice to enter residential care, and the majority are admitted (often with little consultation and sometimes under pressure) as the result of arrangements by someone else. (Booth, 1992:2)

From the little that is known, disabled people living in residential homes tend to have one of four particular medical conditions – multiple sclerosis, cerebral palsy, stroke or rheumatoid arthritis. While this is reflective of the whole population of disabled people, those with multiple sclerosis form a disproportionately high (over half) part of the population of health authority YDUs while local authority homes seem to cater primarily (about 40 per cent) for people with cerebral palsy (Leat, 1988). Both the increase in likelihood of residential care with age and the prependency of certain impairments amongst residential home residents, can perhaps be accounted for by dominant social attitudes towards the provision of welfare. Dalley (1996) argues that residential care reflects the ideological attitudes of society as to what form care should take at any particular time. It appears, however, that the application of this ideology may be selective according to medical conditions. This then suggests that people with particular types of impairments may be more vulnerable to being institutionalised as are older disabled people.

Dalley considers, however, that the current climate is in favour of home care, and indeed there has been a gradual acknowledgement that the most appropriate place to live with a disability is in the community, even for those people with severe disabilities. Alf Morris, in opening the Sunningdale conference on disability in the late 1970s, gave voice to this view when he said that 'Happily more and more people are coming to see that it is undesirable to institutionalise even severely disabled people, that their needs must increasingly be met in the community'. This philosophy was enshrined in official documents (DHSS, 1976, 1981) and endorsed in reports like the Snowdon Report, and given parliamentary approval through a series of legal measures, notably the Chronically Sick and Disabled Persons Act 1970.

This change of attitude may be insufficient in itself, though, to replace the physical legacy of centuries of development of institutions. Furthermore, while the rhetoric of community care may be dominant, in practice there has been a massive growth in residential provision since 1948 when the NHS inherited just 55 000 beds for chronically sick people from the Poor Law infirmaries and workhouses (Barnes, 1991). By 1996 there were 506 500 places in residential and nursing homes, excluding YDUs, housing just over 428 000 people (Department of Health, 1996). Langan (1990) argued that the current community care legislation which encourages the expansion of the independent sector would continue to cause the growth of institutional care as it is more profitable than any of the alternatives.

This is borne out in two ways. First, local authorities have set community care spending limits relative to the cost of residential and nursing homes, which thus provides an institutional norm to the cost of caring and sets inappropriate limits on what will be paid to maintain someone in the community. It is possible for disabled people at risk of entering residential care who are aged 16 to 65 years, and who are in receipt of the higher rate Disability Living Allowance, and who are receiving at least £200 worth of services from the local authority, to apply to the Independent Living (1993) Fund. This, however, places a total limit of £500 per week on the combined local authority and ILF package which is considerably less than what may be spent by those authorities on some specialist nursing homes. Second, local authorities have a duty to promote the independent sector and currently have to spend 85 per cent of the funds transferred to them under the NHS and Community Care Act in this area, thereby ensuring that community care remains a supply, not demand-led service. The Department of Health (1996) statistics suggest, however, that there has been little change in the overall numbers of physically disabled people housed in residential homes since this data was first collected in 1987, although the number of residential homes for this specific group of people has increased from 256 in 1986 (Leat, 1988) to 350 in 1996, excluding small homes (those with fewer than four residents).

The continued use of residential care may also be due to personal economic factors. Schorr (1992) points to the correlation that exists, in both Britain and the United States, between the use of residential care and income. It is only when the spending power of elderly people has increased relative to the incomes of others in the population that there has been any reduction in the trend of increasing numbers of people entering residential homes. He argues that changes in welfare policy must include income maintenance issues as well as personal social services policy if community care is to succeed. This was also the position taken in 1976 by the Union of Physically Impaired Against Segregation (UPIAS) in its statement of Fundamental Principles of Disability:

> Of course the Union supports and struggles for increased help for physically impaired people, there can be no doubt about our impoverishment and the need for urgent change. However, our Union's Aims seek the 'necessary financial . . . and other help required from the State to enable us to gain the maximum possible independence in daily living activities, to achieve mobility, undertake productive work and to live where and how we choose with full control over our lives'. (cited in Oliver, 1996:24)

These trends have important ramifications for the shape and future of residential care facilities for disabled people. Some, like the UPIAS, have called for nothing less than the complete disappearance of all segregated and segregative institutions:

> The Union's eventual object is to achieve a situation where as physically impaired people we all have the means to choose where and how we wish to live. This will involve the phasing out of segregated institutions maintained by the State or Charities.

And while stopping short of a demand for closure of all existing institutions, they state that 'The Union is opposed to the building of any further segregated institutions' (UPIAS policy statement, *Disability Challenge*, May 1981). At the same time, however, Topliss was arguing the need for additional residential facilities: 'The real issues are the desperate shortage of facilities and the fact that standards and variety in the provision of residential accommodation are not commensurate with expectations and variety of needs of disabled individuals' (in Topliss and Gould, 1981:118). However, in 1996 the Department of Health (1996) statistics showed that there were about 900 vacant places (just over 8 per cent of the total) in residential homes for physically/sensorily disabled people which suggests that this type of provision is grossly over-supplied. Although overall numbers of residents may not have been increasing over this period, the growth in numbers of homes may be problematic if the purchasing of services remains supply-led.

Residential care for all client groups has been heavily criticised for many years and this is equally true in respect of disabled people. From the perspective of the social model of disability there is little doubt that the experience of residential care further disables impaired individuals. Before considering the implications of the social model and the possible tasks of social workers in relation to independent living, it is necessary to fill out some of the background to residential care, outline some of the criticisms of it and then consider some of the alternatives.

The legal situation of residential care

Social services departments have a duty under part III, section 21, of the National Assistance Act 1948 'to provide residential accommodation for persons who by reason of age, illness, disability or any other circumstances are in need of care and attention which is not otherwise available to them', and they must also 'have regard for the welfare of all persons for whom such accommodation is provided'. Despite subsequent amendment, in particular by the NHS and Community Care Act 1990, the statutory duty remains though it must now be achieved through purchasing the majority of such services from the private and voluntary sectors.

The 1948 Act recognised a powerful historical tradition for charitable agencies to be involved in such provision and thereby permitted local authorities to delegate their powers to approved agencies if they so wished. Some authorities chose to do this, and the largest agency providing residential accommodation for disabled people was the Leonard Cheshire Foundation, which has a network of over 70 Cheshire homes throughout Britain. The NHS also has responsibility for providing residential accommodation for disabled people and its powers in this area stem from section 12 of the Health Services and Public Health Act 1968 and section 2 of the National Health Service Reorganisation Act 1973. These powers enable the NHS to provide residential accommodation for physically handicapped people in units which are usually YDUs, but the medical emphasis is often retained, even in the title when they are called 'young chronic sick units'.

While the first of these units was opened in 1968, the building programme for new units was accelerated after the passage of the Chronically Sick and Disabled Persons Act 1970, for section 17 requires that:

> In any hospital a person who is suffering from a condition of chronic illness or disability is not cared for in the hospital as an in-patient in any part of the hospital which is normally used wholly or mainly for the care of elderly persons, unless he is himself an elderly person.

According to one national survey (Bloomfield, 1976) there were 41 operational YDUs in Britain in 1975 in comparison with 30 purpose-built local authority homes (Goldsmith, 1976). By 1986 the figures had risen to 72 YDUs and 58 local authority homes (Leat, 1988). In the early 1980s, both social services and health authorities had plans for a considerable number of additional units but economic circumstances and consumer resistance slowed down building programmes. This was effectively halted by the amendment to the supplementary benefit regulations regarding board and lodging payments in 1983 which led to a massive increase in the number of private residential and nursing homes. This change permitted the then DHSS to pay the fees for people in voluntary and private residential and nursing homes, thereby transferring much of the responsibility for these costs away from local authorities and the NHS. These payments eventually constituted the sums that were transferred from the Department of Social Security to local authorities under the NHS and Community Care Act 1990, placing the responsibility for all residential and nursing home funding with social services departments.

There are effectively three main sectors providing residential accommodation for disabled people: local authorities, the health service and the independent sector including voluntary organisations such as the Cheshire Foundation and a large number of private homes. There is no clear distinction between them, and while some are registered as residential homes under the Registered Homes Act 1984, others are registered as nursing homes under the same Act. In practice those establishments registered as nursing homes are able to charge higher fees, and while they theoretically may take people requiring greater levels of assistance this is not necessarily the case. Small homes, those with fewer than four residents, have also been required to register since 1993 under the Registered Homes (Amendment) Act 1991.

Residential accommodation for disabled people: a provision under attack

Since the publication of *Asylums* (Goffman, 1961) a considerable amount of work on the effects of institutionalisation has been done. 'Total institutions', as Goffman called them, are characterised by a loss of privacy, a lack of freedom of choice, and the individual within them misses the opportunity to make meaningful personal relationships. The institution provides a highly structured routine where the lives of the individual residents are regulated by management and all tend to be treated alike. This gives rise to what has been identified as institutional neurosis:

> a disease characterised by apathy, lack of initiative, loss of interest more marked in things and events not immediately personal or present, submissiveness, and sometimes no expression of feelings or resentment at harsh or unfair orders. There is also a lack of interest in the future and an apparent inability to make practical plans for it, a deterioration in personal habits, toilet and standards generally, a loss of individuality, and a resigned acceptance that things will go on as they are – unchangingly, inevitably and indefinitely. (Barton, 1959)

Such studies as are specifically concerned with institutions for disabled people have tended to see the effects of institution-alisation on the residents in less dramatic terms than Goffman. The 'warehousing' model of residential care described by Miller and Gwynne (1971) in *A Life Apart*, and which they call the conventional approach to residential care, approximates to Goffman's total institution in its requirement that the inmate remains dependent and depersonalised and subjugated to the task of the institution. The authors were 'captured by the plight of intelligent cripples . . . who were forced to lead stunted lives in institutions that do not provide opportunities for their development'. But they do not portray the residents they met in the negative terms used by Barton, for instance; two poss-ible differences are that schizophrenic patients studied by Barton are particularly vulnerable to institutionalisation and that the psychiatric hospital is more of a 'closed' community than the residential home for disabled people. In another study of a home for disabled people, Musgrove (1977) describes a visit to a Cheshire home, which he saw as fitting Goffman's pic-ture of a total institution only in a very superficial way, as the residents were not completely regimented, and he was struck, contrary to his expectation, by the extent to which they had managed to maintain their sense of identity.

However, in a view from the inside (as opposed to Musgrove's outsider view), Battye, who experienced life as a resident in both the chronic ward of a long-stay hospital and a Cheshire home, saw the difference between the two, in spite of the more favourable lifestyle of the latter, as one only of degree, not of kind:

Unless he fights a constant battle to retain his intellectual integrity and sense of purpose, as the years go by he will gradually feel the atmosphere of the place closing in on him as it did in the chronic ward . . . in spite of efforts to arouse or retain his interest in life he will feel boredom and apathy creeping over him like a slow paralysis eroding his will, dulling his critical wits, dousing his spirit, killing his independence . . . In a subtler, more civilised way than in the chronic ward, he will have become institutionalised. (Battye, 1966:14)

Miller and Gwynne (1971) in their study of local authority and voluntary homes drew the distinction between 'warehousing' and 'horticultural' models of residential care. The warehousing model expresses the humanitarian or medical value that the prolongation of life is a good thing but the question concerning the purpose of the life that is prolonged is never asked. The emphasis is on medical care and the minimisation of risk – the main aim is to keep the gap between social death (the point when the disabled person enters the institution) and physical death as long as possible. Alternatively, the horticultural model emphasises the uniqueness of each inmate, the importance of individual responsibility, and the potential to realise unfulfilled ambitions and capacities.

However, Miller and Gwynne (1971) failed to fully endorse the horticultural model because of their concerns that it was problematic due to the overvaluing of independence, the denial of disability and the distortion of staff–resident relations where the real facts of the situation are ignored or distorted. There have been few attempts to implement completely the horticultural model and no evaluations of its effectiveness, although impressionistic evidence from one residential home (Dartington *et al.*, 1981) which operated broadly within this model endorsed Hunt's (1981) view that, 'The liberal growth approach, whatever criticisms may be made of some of its theories and assumptions, represents a genuine advance towards securing the rights and freedoms of a civilised life for many handicapped people'. Hunt and other residents of Le Court quickly came to realise that regardless of changes that might be made to the operation of residential homes, the process of segregation would continue to be a process of social death that could only be countered by living options that were integrated within the community.

It is not just voluntary and local authority homes which have come in for such criticism but YDUs also. Bloomfield in her national survey argues:

> While it cannot be denied that many of the inmates of Younger Chronic Sick Units require extensive help with personal care, it is refuted that this help can only be provided in a hospital setting. By focusing on this one aspect of the

inmates' requirements, the Younger Chronic Sick Unit systematically robs the individual of the opportunity for achieving satisfaction and purpose in the life remaining to him. The unavoidable emphasis on his physical dependence on authoritative personnel frequently leads all but the strongest individuals to an accepting, apathetic state with little interest in life and even less initiative. (Bloomfield, 1976)

When the health authority in Rochdale attempted to build a YDU, it met with such resistance that it had to abandon their plans (Finlay, 1978), and the same happened in Surrey (North Surrey CHC, 1978). Internal and external criticisms of the residential care sector coupled with consumer resistance have forced providers to look to possible alternatives, but despite a few changes the numbers of disabled people entering residential care remains constant as do the criticisms. Laurie summarises the attitudes of many disabled people towards residential care:

> Residential institutions can become virtual prisons for disabled people if and when denied any choice in daily decisions – what to eat and when, when to get up and go to bed, who provides assistance and how that is provided. Thus, residents in institutions often find themselves stripped of their privacy, dignity and individuality with no locks on bathroom or bedroom doors, staff entering rooms without knocking, and the right to form relationships denied. (Laurie, 1991:51)

The social-model analysis of institutionalised care, both in segregated homes and in the community, has highlighted the issue of violence towards disabled people. Just as children are made vulnerable to abuse by being placed in institutions, disabled adults have also become victims of criminal assaults and of other acts of violence that are not deemed illegal by society. In a Canadian study of violence towards disabled people the Roeher Institute found that:

> people with disabilities are more likely than others to be subjected to acts of violence and abuse that are

proscribed by criminal and civil acts. They are also subjected to acts of violence and abuse that do not meet legal
definitions of violence but that the survivors perceive as
harmful. These may include acts that are perpetrated in
places where the abuse is shielded from the arm of the law.
Contributing to the vulnerability is society's inability or
unwillingness to clearly name and prohibit the problem. But
equally important are the often radically unequal social and
economic position[s] of persons with disabilities that place
them at a disproportionate risk, as well as the lack of individual control and choice that makes it difficult for the individual to avoid and escape situations of risk. (Rioux *et al.*,
1997:203)

Many criticisms of residential care implicitly and explicitly
draw upon the social model of disability in that they see institutional regimes as adding to rather than alleviating many
of the problems that disabled individuals face, but in terms
of translating this into an active social policy there are some
pitfalls in the alternatives.

Alternative models of living to residential care

The disabled village

This is based on the village settlement at Het Dorp in Hol-
land where around 400 severely disabled people were accom-
modated in one colony. Approximately 80 per cent of the
residents were single but there were a number of married
couples where both parties were severely impaired. Each resident had a self-contained flat, and services such as meals and
staff care were provided on site.

The argument in favour of this sort of development is that
it does allow severely handicapped residents to take control
of their own lives. However, the village was not successfully
integrated into the wider community and it became a 'cripples' colony' with little mixing of disabled and non-disabled
people. There are a couple of similar settlements in Britain,
most notably the Thistle Foundation Village in Edinburgh and

the Papworth Settlement in Cambridgeshire. The idea of villages is probably discredited for people with physical impairments but there are still those who would advocate that they are suitable for people with learning difficulties.

Collective houses

A number of these have sprung up in Denmark whereby the tenancies of blocks of flats are allocated on the approximate ratio of one disabled person to three non-disabled ones. Consumer services such as restaurants are contained within the blocks and the aim was to move away from institutions and colonies. Unfortunately, this ratio has tended to be rather high and internal social divisions between disabled and non-disabled people have occurred. Additionally, the outside world has continued to regard those houses as institutions for the disabled.

While collective houses have not developed on a large scale outside Denmark, there have been a few isolated experiments in Britain where severely disabled people have lived in flats where other non-disabled tenants provided physical assistance in exchange for lower rents. Probably the most successful example of this kind of development, though on a smaller scale than the Danish collective houses, is the Grove Road scheme (Davis, 1981). Not only did it provide an appropriate housing environment, but the disabled people were able to manage with less than one-third of the direct physical assistance that they had needed while in residential care, and they were also able to prove wrong all of the professional assessments which had labelled them 'too disabled to live in the community'.

Fokus housing

This has developed in Sweden and has been an attempt to integrate severely disabled people into ordinary housing schemes. Supportive services are provided and there are a range of communal facilities available. It is estimated that in 1983 there were over 2000 severely disabled people living in this type of accommodation in Sweden.

While these schemes have moved a long way towards integration of disabled people, it has been suggested that some of the trappings of institutionalisation remain and that not all of the tenants become part of the community. Ratzka (1991) argues that not only do individual disabled people have no choice in who provides their personal assistance in these schemes, but that the lack of control over when it will be provided means that Fokus is based on the 'house arrest principle' of care.

In Britain, following the Chronically Sick and Disabled Persons Act 1970, many housing authorities attempted to integrate housing for disabled people into their new schemes. However, such disabled people rely on community medical and nursing services for support, and these are often too remote or inflexible to allow severely impaired people to live in the community without a great deal of family support. Furthermore, since the late 1970s policy towards public sector housing led to a rapid decline in construction and has effectively ended this programme.

British housing association schemes

The early examples of these were assemblies of between 12 and 25 flats grouped together to form a 'mini-colony', often with a warden or caretaker to oversee the residents. These were usually built in an urban setting and close to the main services and were purpose-designed to maximise independent living. There are a number of examples of this type of provision including Friendship House at Poole built by the Raglan Housing Association, and Princes Crescent, Finsbury Park built by the John Grooms Housing Association.

It is interesting to note that some of the most important voluntary organisations in the residential care sector have set up their own housing associations to provide suitable accommodation in the community – notably the Spastics Society, John Grooms and the Cheshire Foundation. While many of these schemes may have removed the worst effects of institutionalisation, it was been suggested that they did not truly integrate disabled people into the community, but rather provided a more sympathetic, though still isolated, physical environment. Thus they only go some way towards removing the disabling effects of institutionalisation.

Housing associations have however, become the major source of new accessible dwellings for disabled people, and some such as Habinteg have been commended for their good practice (Laurie, 1991). Habinteg build integrated estates in which approximately 25 per cent of properties are wheelchair accessible while others are all built to a mobility standard. They also avoid the mistake of only building single-bedroomed properties, recognising that disabled people have and are part of families. However, it must also be recognised that this has not been the pattern of either housing association or local authority building (Morris, 1990) and that inappropriate policies and practices concerning the size, nature and location of properties may be major factors in the fact that only 24 per cent of lettings of housing association wheelchair dwellings in 1996 were to wheelchair users (Harris *et al.*, 1997).

Lifetime homes

Lifetime homes describes a standard of building which means that all housing would have the potential to be adapted for use by a disabled person. The standard was first recommended by the United Nations in 1974 and yet in Europe only Italy, the Netherlands, Spain, Sweden and Norway have adopted it and only Norway offers any incentives through building loans (Ambrose, 1997). Recent studies in the UK (Bonnett, 1996; Cobbold, 1997) have shown that this policy would be cost-effective and the Labour government elected in 1997 have stated that they will introduce these standards into building regulations in 1999. When this happens it will increase the opportunities of independent living for disabled people by widening their choice in housing.

Personal assistance schemes

These are schemes where individual disabled people obtain cash payments from the state in order to directly employ others to act as personal assistants to them. In 1988 the Independent Living Fund (ILF) was set up which gave large numbers of disabled people access to funds for this purpose, and in 1993 this responsibility was absorbed by local authorities following implementation of the NHS and Community Care Act 1990. In support of this trend, the Greenwich Association of Disabled People (GAD) employed a Personal Assistance Advisor to help individuals with the problems they might encounter by taking on an employment role. An evaluation of this scheme found that after three years of operating that its success was such that:

> developing independent living options like Personal Assistance Schemes is not just morally desirable and professionally appropriate, but also offers the possibility of providing more cost effective and efficient services through switching from the overproduction of services that people don't want or need and the underproduction of those that they do, to a situation where the services that are produced and purchased by statutory providers are precisely the services that users want and need. (Oliver and Zarb, 1992:13).

The Community Care (Direct Payments) Act 1996 makes it possible for local authorities to support individual personal assistance schemes with cash payments to disabled people rather than providing them with services. This does then help to overcome many of the problems experienced in relation to the provision of adequate support services within the housing schemes mentioned above. However, the transfer of employer responsibilities from local authorities to individual disabled people also requires a transfer of skills in the recruitment, management and administration of the service. A very useful guide to setting up such schemes has been written by Simpson and Campbell (1996) and is aimed at helping disabled people, voluntary organisations and social services staff understand what these responsibilities are and how to undertake them.

Social work, the social model and residential care

The social model suggests that disability is imposed upon impaired individuals as a consequence of the way society is organised. There can be little doubt that residential care in most cases does indeed further disable impaired individuals, and from this viewpoint residential care offers an unacceptable form of provision, at least as it is presently organised.

It is easy to see how by working within the individual model of disability, those involved in planning and providing services for disabled people are led to see residential provision as a suitable option when an individual is no longer able to continue living as previously, either as a consequence of family break up, lack of community support and/or increasing impairment. The question for those charged with responsibility for providing a service from within the individual model then automatically becomes: what does the individual need? The answer logically is food, clothing, shelter and personal assistance, and when individual needs are aggregated it seems not unreasonable to meet these needs through the provision of residential accommodation for a number of individuals, especially given the social and economic pressures from the care industry to make such a choice.

The question service providers should ask from within the social model, however, is a different one, and becomes: in what ways does the physical and social environment prevent this individual from remaining in the community and continuing to live an independent life? This obviously produces a different answer along the lines of the need for suitable and adequate housing, a reasonable income to ensure access to food, clothing and personal assistance, the provision of community support, and so on.

The first social work task, then, is to ensure that those who are at risk of being forced to go into residential care are given the option of remaining in the community with adequate support. It is argued that some may wish to go into residential care, and if this is the case it should be a real choice available, but impaired people should not be forced into becoming further disabled because residential care is the only option available or the choice of the authorities. Neither should it be assumed that a disabled person is actually making a free choice if they opt for residential care as this may be an act of desperation following their experience of inadequate support in the community. Also, the argument commonly put forward by local authorities that this is the cheaper option for certain individuals does not itself stand up to scrutiny, given the disproportionately high amount of PSS budgets that is spent on a relatively small proportion of disabled people, and that we know from the evidence that the local authority community schemes against which this is compared are themselves overpriced and wasteful (Oliver and Zarb, 1992). The social services department and the social worker must aim to provide a range of options which maximises choice, and some of the alternatives discussed should be considered instead of building or funding yet more homes along traditional lines.

Having said that, there are many people already in residential care and social workers may have a role to play in working with them. Thus 'physically or mentally handicapped people in residential care may not only require good physical care, but they may also need help to overcome the effects their respective disabilities may have upon their personal and social lives and relationships' (Payne, 1978:60).

These disabilities, following the social model, are a consequence of the institutionalisation of people and not a result of their impairments, and consequently solutions may involve some or all of the following:

1. The demedicalisation of residential care with a move away from matrons, doctors, nursing staff and uniforms, and in particular with regard to YDUs the separation of them from hospitals. The introduction of rigorous health and safety procedures following the AIDs scare in the 1980s affects all people but should not be taken to a level where it acts to dehumanise what has become an individual's own home. What is perhaps more pertinent in most registered homes is the level of instrumental 'quality assurance' procedures by which they demonstrate their standards. These can be so intrusive and demanding on staff time that they prevent many other services from being provided and illustrate the extent to which the real cost of such provision remains hidden.

2. Increasing the privacy and autonomy of individual residents through recognition of their civil rights. This includes providing single rooms with *en suite* bathing and toilet facili-

ties, and ensuring choice remains with the disabled person when deciding who provides them with personal assistance so that all residents can have access to privacy. People should not be prevented from locking their own doors, providing their own furniture and living in the style they choose, including making their own decisions about when to go to bed, to get up, and what meals to eat and where to eat them.

3. Developing more constructive activities including access to gainful employment and ensuring residents have control over ordinary living activities such as cooking, washing, ironing and cleaning in terms of how, when and by whom they are done.

4. Ensuring there are no barriers to accessing the outside world. Although the mobility allowance, now the mobility component of the DLA, has gone some way towards making this easier, there are obvious difficulties for those homes deep in the countryside and some homes continue to take these additional payments from their residents. Furthermore, residents in YDUs may not be allowed out unaccompanied due to NHS regulations and others may find themselves living in a 'house arrest' situation as described in the Swedish experience earlier. Neither of these are acceptable policies and social workers should seriously question their own participation in the effective detainment of disabled people when their legal duty is towards their welfare.

5. Bringing the outside world in, though this should only be done at the behest of the residents, for there is nothing more degrading and depersonalising than conducted tours by local dignitaries of what, after all, are people's homes. Everyone, disabled or not, surely has the right to decide who can enter their own homes and people in residential care must be accorded that same basic right.

6. Ensuring that disabled people can feel secure and safe from acts of violence and abuse within their home. This requires those in positions of responsibility, including social workers, to listen and act when disabled people are reporting violence. In Britain, courts may reject the ability of disabled people to give evidence because of their impairments. This was illustrated in a case in 1997 in Birmingham when

a woman with multiple sclerosis was declared an incompetent witness in a case against a care worker who was accused of serious assault because she could not talk and the judge refused to hear evidence in any other manner. Once again, social workers must not collude by paying for services that are in reality abusive.

These suggestions offer achievable ways of improving the lives of those currently in residential care. And of course they do not preclude the provision of counselling services as well, for some residents may indeed wish, and need, to have access to that kind of therapeutic relationship. However, it would be an unfortunate mistake to attempt to provide personal counselling for all residents without questioning the need for improvements within the institution itself or the need to help those wishing to escape it. Above all else, residential care staff and social workers have a duty to assist those disabled people who are living in segregated establishments by making the alternatives available so that disabled people can realistically develop the self-confidence to leave.

The immediate possibility of leaving an institution may not be available to all people for a variety of reasons, so another social work task might therefore be to protect vulnerable people from the disabling consequences of their environments over a long period of time. Shearer indicts social workers for failing so to do with regard to disabled children on the 'special care' wards of hospitals:

> The social workers who might have been expected to show concern for the appalling standards of child-care on the wards commonly saw this as none of their concern: one had nothing to do with them because 'these children will never be discharged'. (Shearer, 1981a:102)

There is obviously a dilemma for social workers who think they desperately need a residential place for clients but are less than happy with what is available. While there are no easy answers, it is worth remembering that local authorities pay fees for such accommodation, and the social worker as the representative of the authority is entitled to have a say.

There is one further issue to consider and that concerns the additional functions of residential care, which does not exist solely to meet the needs of residents. Goffman drew attention to this when he wrote:

> If all the institutions in a given region were emptied and closed down today, tomorrow parents, relatives, police, judges, doctors and social workers would raise a clamour for new ones: and these the true clients of the institution would demand new institutions to satisfy their needs. (Goffman, 1961:334)

In the last chapter it was suggested that physical impairment disables other family members, particularly spouses or daughters, and residential care is increasingly being used on a short-term basis in order to give carers a break. In many cases the disabled person is perfectly prepared to go into care on a short-term basis, but some refuse and this may place the social worker in a dilemma: Who should be regarded as the client?

Whose needs should take precedence? If more community support were available it might be possible to provide the carer with a break without resort to residential care; if residential care were better, people might enter into it more willingly. Ultimately, however, the social worker may be faced with attempts to reconcile conflicting interests, and such work will inevitably require a long-term casework approach with the whole family if the ultimate outcome of permanent residential care and complete family break up is to be avoided.

Day-care facilities

One important resource available to the social worker and the disabled person which may prevent family break up and admittance to residential care is the day-centre. By going to a day-centre on a regular basis, the stresses and strains can be alleviated in the carer and the disabled person can also receive a wider range of experiences than would otherwise be available. However, as with residential care, there are a number of criticisms that can be levelled at day care which call into question the extent of its usefulness.

One criticism is that day-centres are themselves often segregative, and while most of the buildings may be located in urban settings their use is often restricted to the 'client group'. Many centres organise their activities around the idea of work, though those participating are not paid a wage. This has led some critics to state that:

> To expect disabled people to do boring work and to do it for a pittance does seem to smack of exploitation ... We consider that thirty hours a week packing greasy gaskets for a mere £2 or so is the modern equivalent of oakum-picking, with some of the same thinking behind it. (Tuckey and Tuckey, 1981:12)

Defenders of such activities point to two things in its favour: they suggest that for many users 'proper work', even for a pittance, is more rewarding than middle-class activities like basket-making, painting and craft work; they further argue that even if they wanted to pay more money this is impossible because social security regulations will not allow it and also many disabled people do not do enough work to 'earn' the money.

The real criticism of centres based upon work is that the need to fulfil contracts and meet target dates often dominates the life of centres and prevents sufficient attention being given to other needs and activities. Furthermore, such contracts are usually negotiated by centre managers or other departmental staff and not by the disabled clientele themselves. This leads to another criticism of such centres, even those organised around the idea of 'care': that is, that they are essentially paternalistic, and in the majority of cases disabled people are the passive recipients of day-care services. In short, impaired people are often further disabled by the regimes of the day-centres available to them.

Day care, then, like residential care, can be criticised on a number of grounds and this obviously poses a dilemma for the social worker wishing to use it as a resource. Should people be referred to a centre where the regime is seen as being unacceptable, or should the need of the carer for a break be regarded as paramount? Of course, neither extreme position needs to be taken and it is perfectly possible to place some-one in a centre while pressing for changes in the organisa-tion and functioning of the centre at the same time. Indeed, some day-centres have attempted to change by becoming re-source centres which provide advisory services and may even have developed user-control mechanisms. Tuckey and Tuckey (1981) provide a descriptive account of the kind of day-centre that is more appropriate to the needs of disabled people, and indeed compatible with the social model of disability, a centre whose title (*An Ordinary Place*) encapsulates its basic philo-sophy. However, there is still a long way to go in removing the segregationalist ideology that underpins the vast majority of such provision.

Social work and independent living

Residential and day care are two of the resources available to people living with disabilities and to social workers who may be involved with them. However, there are two basic ques-tions which hang over both kinds of resource, from the point of view of both providers and users: How appropriate are such resources? What can be done to improve them? While some answers have been given to the latter, these can only ever amount to the treatment of symptoms rather than the cause, which is the use of such services in the first place. What is required of social workers is that they first understand the meaning and implications of independent living and, second, that they use their skills and their role within the welfare sys-tem to support disabled people in pursuit of this.

While many models of care have been provided over the years, the key to independent living is that full control of the provision of personal assistance should be handed over to the disabled person who is to receive it. Within the new mar-ket structures of welfare in Britain, this means giving disabled people the finances to resource their own personal assistance schemes and then supporting them in the task in ways that they determine as being of use.

As local authorities begin to implement the Community Care (Direct Payments) Act 1996, social workers and care managers will be required to relinquish part of their responsibility for the purchasing or provision of community care services and to support individuals in running their own personal assistance schemes. Just as senior managers and councillors have found it difficult to delegate the responsibility for budgets to caseworkers as was envisaged in the earlier white paper, *Caring for People* (Department of Health, 1989), they will probably resist handing over such responsibility to disabled people. The immediate task of the social worker, therefore, will be one of working with disabled people to put the case for this change within their agencies. If social workers are committed to the delivery of non-stigmatised services, then this piece of legislation probably offers them their best opportunity since 1948 to humanise the relationship between disabled people and the state.

Once its implementation has been achieved, it will be for social workers to ensure that the administration of these monies, and the ways in which disabled people are required to account for their use, is managed in a manner that is helpful to the aims of independent living and not in ways that replicate the barriers of institutionalised care.

6

The Legal and Social Context of Disability

Living within a family or in residential accommodation can be disabling for impaired people, and in the wider context all impaired people are disabled to a greater or lesser degree by the society in which they live. The social model of disability suggests that impaired people in Britain may face educational disability, employment disability and economic disability, and it is perhaps somewhat ironic that some of the legal measures taken to combat such disadvantages actually further contribute to the disabling process. This chapter will focus upon some aspects of this relationship between disabled people and society and consider some of the possible intervention strategies for social workers. To begin with the discussion needs to be placed in the context of legislation relating to disability.

The legal rights of disabled people

While it is indeed possible to trace state involvement and concern with physically disabled people back to 1601 and beyond, there is little need to go back further than the 1940s, when the foundations of the welfare state were laid. Prior to this, statutory provision for disabled people had been made on a piecemeal or *ad hoc* basis and often only related to specific types of disability or the way in which disabilities had been caused. While this specificity has not been completely eradicated, state provision is now geared towards disabled people as a single group.

The first Act of Parliament to treat disabled people as one single category of persons was the Disabled Persons (Employment)

Act 1944. Not only did this attempt to ensure that employers employed a certain number of disabled workers but it also made provision for the assessment of employment potential, the establishment of rehabilitation centres and the provision of vocational training courses and maintenance grants for those selected to attend them. Subsequently the National Health Service Act 1946, while providing for the acute medical needs of disabled people, also made it possible for local authority health departments to provide any medical equipment or aids necessary to keep people in their own homes. The National Assistance Act 1948 made some provision for meeting the financial needs of disabled people and in addition imposed a duty on local authorities to provide residential accommodation and services for 'persons who are blind, deaf or dumb and other persons who are substantially and permanently handicapped by illness, injury or congenital deformity'. This was extended in 1974 by the Secretary of State through Local Authority Circular 13/74 to include 'persons suffering from a mental disorder of any description'. In addition the Education Act 1944 stated that every child should receive education suitable for his age, ability and aptitude and to provide special educational treatment for those thought to need it.

These Acts formed the cornerstone of statutory provision for disabled people and with the exception of the Disability Discrimination Act 1995 which represents a different approach to disability issues, particularly employment, subsequent legislation has merely altered, modified or extended existing provision. The current situation regarding education and employment will be discussed separately as will discrimination, but to begin with consideration needs to be given to the provision of social welfare.

Perhaps the most important and certainly the most publicised piece of legislation in this area is the Chronically Sick and Disabled Persons Act 1970. This sought to give disabled people the right to live in the community, by providing appropriate support services. Section 1 of the Act imposes two duties on local authorities:

(a) the duty to inform themselves of the number and needs of handicapped persons in their areas

(b) the duty to publicise available services

The latter of these originally only applied to those services provided by the local authority itself, but this was extended by the Disabled Persons (Services, Consultation and Representation) Act 1986 to include any services known to them.

Further, section 2 lists various services which should be provided for those whose needs have been assessed, and these may include:

(a) practical assistance in the home
(b) recreational facilities both in the home and outside
(c) travel facilities, either free or subsidised
(d) social work support to families
(e) adaptations to the home and special equipment including telephones
(f) holiday arrangements
(g) meals

Since the Children Act 1989 these services only apply to adults.

The 1970 Act was regarded by some (Topliss and Gould, 1981) as nothing less than 'a charter for the disabled', its very presence constituting nothing less than public acknowledgement of the social rights of disabled people. However, the evidence for this is somewhat tenuous, and Topliss and Gould argue that:

> Society may in fact have expended too little in the way of resources and effort to adjust the environment, as much as many would wish, to meet the needs of disabled people, but the acceptance of an obligation to move in this direction has never been challenged since the passing of the Act. (Topliss and Gould, 1981:142)

It is further claimed that the passage of the Act and its subsequent presence have also increased public awareness of disability and changed attitudes towards disabled people. Finally, it is often claimed that the Act at last laid down a statutory framework for services to which disabled people were entitled.

There are a number of criticisms that can be levelled at this evaluation of the Act. To begin with, one commentator has noted that 'In the main, Section 2 of the Chronically Sick and Disabled Persons Act . . . is only Section 29 of the National Assistance Act 1948 writ large' (Keeble, 1979:40). It has also been claimed that the Act was a watershed in the lives of disabled people, and undoubtedly there has been a very real improvement in services in the last few decades. However, criticism has been noted of the Act in that it 'appears to make a lot of highly satisfactory promises but careful analysis of Section 2 reveals that nothing must of necessity be provided outright, let alone free' (ibid.:41).

There has certainly been concern expressed that the Act promises more than it actually delivers and one national survey concluded: 'The CSDPA surveys found handicapped people requiring and wanting help who were not in regular contact with any of the professional caring services and some who, although in contact with one service, needed help from another' (Knight and Warren, 1978:70). Numerous economic crises and subsequent cutbacks have exacerbated these problems as local authorities have often withdrawn services previously provided.

Another criticism often made (Shearer, 1981b; Knight and Warren, 1978) is that services are often provided on the basis of locality rather than on need. There is considerable variability between local authorities about what services they provide and, unfortunately, it is still true that the best professional advice for some disabled people is to 'move'! This problem was perhaps best summed up in the title of Feidler's (1988) report for the Prince of Wales Advisory Group on Disability, *Living Options Lottery*.

Another serious criticism of the 1970 Act stems from the RADAR project undertaken by 15 major disability organisations which attempted to clarify the law regarding this particular piece of legislation (Cook and Mitchell, 1982). One of the major flaws that had arisen with the CSDPA was that local authorities argued that while they may have a duty to provide services to meet an individual's need, they did not if they were unaware of that need. Their tactic was to delay assessment until resources were available. Despite some limited success in individual cases which was accounted for by the local authorities taking action to avoid a precedent-setting court case, it was clear that given the current economic climate and the often uneasy relationship between central and local government, the Act was neither implementable nor enforceable. The position was to some extent corrected by section 4 of the 1986 Act which clarified beyond doubt the local authority's responsibility to carry out an assessment if requested to do so by either a disabled person or her/his carer, while sections 5 and 6 laid down detailed procedures for children with special educational needs to be assessed under the 1970 Act when they reached school leaving age.

What remained unresolved was the extent of the duty to provide services. As the 1970 Act had begun life as a private member's bill, it could not constitutionally cause local authorities to incur additional costs. However, a Money Order Resolution passed by the government did make provision for this but it remained unclear as to the extent of the duty (Topliss and Gould, 1981). The position was clarified by the NHS and Community Care Act 1990 which placed clear budgetary limits on all local authority spending in relation to both residential/nursing homes and community care. The duty to provide services is now restricted by the budget although it remains somewhat unclear as to the extent to which local authorities can internally ring-fence their resources.

Finally, Shearer (1981b) is not just critical of the Act's failure to meet need and provide services, but also of its underlying philosophy, which, she suggests, takes away from disabled people the crucial element of choice:

> The offer of a holiday at a time and in a place that suits the social service worker or local authority, rather than cash in hand to spend according to individual preference, sits oddly with the rhetoric which asserts that people with disabilities should have greater access to the range of social choices that many of the rest of society take for granted. The substitution of kind for cash sits no less uneasily with aspirations to enhance the self-determination and dignity of people with disabilities, in a society where status and respect has so much to do with purchasing power. The potential public outcry against a paternalistic state which

attempted to deliver, say, child benefit in the form of nappies, creams and baby foods, does not take much imagining. (Shearer, 1981b:82–3)

All the above criticisms remain valid despite the passing and implementation of the National Health Service and Community Care Act 1990, which certainly claimed the intent to tackle many of them. The needs-led assessment which is central to the 1990 Act was intended to get away from the 'MOT test' approach (Middleton, 1992) of section 2 of the CSDPA, while specifying financial responsibilities and charging arrangements were supposed to clarify rights to services. Legislating for collaboration between agencies was also meant to ensure that the gaps between services were plugged and that people could make use of single points of entry into the welfare system. None of these have proved effective as the new focus on budgets that also accompanied this Act ensured that local authorities and the NHS have now institutionalised their boundaries and made assessment a far more instrumental process.

Following the Audit Commission (1986) report into community care, Kenneth Clarke, then Secretary of State for Health, described the supplementary benefit payments for residential care as offering a 'perverse incentive' to local authorities not to provide alternative services. In 1997, after four and a half years of the Act that was supposed to take away those incentives, the Audit Commission reported that the budgetary situation between local authorities and the NHS was like a 'Berlin wall'. Furthermore, charging policies have multiplied since the Act's implementation in 1993, and while the structural inequalities within authorities have lessened those between them have grown. In a direct return to the Poor Law, local authorities even charge each other if the person requiring a service has lived in their area for less than an agreed time limit.

Shearer suggested that the 1970 Act's underlying philosophy was a step in the wrong direction and that what disabled people in fact need is more cash and strong anti-discrimination legislation to ensure that they can buy the kinds of services they need. While neither of these have been achieved in full, both the Community Care (Direct Payments) Act 1996 and the Disability Discrimination Act 1995 have gone some way towards addressing the problem.

The 1996 Act gives local authorities the power, though not a duty, to provide disabled people with the cash to purchase their own community care services. While the assessment of need remains with the local authority, rather than providing or purchasing services to meet that need, they may provide the equivalent in cash which is then used by the disabled person to pay for their own personal assistance. In effect it makes use of the market principles within the 1990 Act but shifts the role of customer from care managers to disabled people. While social workers will retain some responsibility for monitoring the use of this money, they should act in a supportive role, not a policing one. The importance of working with the spirit of this Act was voiced by the Director of the National Centre for Independent Living:

> When the Act comes into force from 1 April 1997 local authorities have been given the choice whether they offer Direct Payments. In my view it will be disastrous if they do not. There is an explicit expectation embodied within the disabled people's movement that Direct Payments will be on offer. All reasoned arguments against it have been demolished throughout the campaign and nowhere better exemplified than on the floor of the House of Commons and the House of Lords where we finally won our victory. It would be a foolish waste of time if we had to repeat that process, because the arguments have been won. (Campbell, 1997:23)

More will be said of anti-discrimination later in the chapter, but it is worth remembering that, whatever its defects, the Chronically Sick and Disabled Persons Act with the subsequent amendments and changes provides a significant part of the legal framework within which social workers, particularly those employed in social services departments, have to work. A crucial problem for social workers (and OTs and other professionals) is that very often they know there are not the resources available to meet the needs they encounter, and yet to acknowledge these needs may well place a legal obligation upon their employer to meet such needs. The problem then centres on differences between administrative and professional definitions of need, and unfortunately most professionals have received little assistance from their own associations in advancing their own professional definitions. It is scarcely credible to imagine doctors refusing to diagnose illnesses because there are not sufficient resources available to treat all those so diagnosed, and other professionals should learn from this self-confidence.

There are a number of informal solutions to this dilemma: social workers may suggest that clients take their complaints to the politicians and can assist by drafting letters themselves. Others have contacted organisations like RADAR and if necessary have done so anonymously. However, while such tactics may resolve discrepancies between need and provision in individual cases, they do not tackle wider issues concerning conflicts between administrative and professional definitions of need, nor do they make the Act ultimately more implementable or enforceable. To be a client (or indeed a social worker) in a service where expectations and needs far outweigh available resources can be a disabling experience in itself. None-the-less, one cannot help feeling that more disabled people would get the services to which they are entitled if professionals were to act as advocates of that need rather than as the rationing agents of their employers.

Education

The Education Act 1944 laid a duty on local authorities to have regard 'to the need for securing that provision is made for pupils who suffer from any disability of the mind and body by providing, either in special schools or otherwise, special educational treatment'. It also obliged the authorities to ascertain the numbers of children in their areas who required special educational treatment. The Act was important for disabled children and their families in that it gave them legal rights to education, but unfortunately it left it to the authorities and to professionals to determine exactly what kind of education was appropriate.

Even more unfortunately, responsible authorities have chosen to make provision for the special needs of disabled children in segregated establishments of one kind or another. Despite

Table 6.1 *Numbers and percentage of school population in special schools*

Year	Numbers	Percentage
1950	47 000	0.75
1955	58 000	0.81
1960	66 000	0.86
1965	74 000	0.96
1970	87 000	1.01
1975	132 000	1.37
1980	130 000	1.45
1985	116 000	1.46
1989	102 000	1.35

Source: Booth (1981:293) and Barnes (1991:39).

mounting criticism of special education over many years, both on the grounds of its failure to provide an adequate or comparable education to that provided in ordinary schools, and the social implications of segregating large numbers of children from their peers, the percentage of the school population in special schools grew steadily until the mid-1980s as Table 6.1 clearly shows. Furthermore, as was noted in Chapter 4, the apparent reduction since 1985 is misleading as it does not reflect the local variations in practice where some authorities have increased the proportion of children they send to special schools by as much as 25 per cent (Barnes, 1991).

In recognition of the growing controversies surrounding the educational needs of disabled children, the government set up a Committee of Enquiry which produced the Warnock Report in 1978. The Report made numerous recommendations, including replacing the original categories of disabled children with the broader concept of 'special educational needs' and the government issued a White Paper in 1980 called *Special Needs in Education* which broadly endorsed the proposals of the Warnock Report. While Warnock, the White Paper and the subsequent 1981 Education Act favoured the idea of integration, no extra resources were made available to facilitate such a move. The 1981 Act left the legal rights of parents and their disabled children unchanged and it was still the local authority which decided what educational provision was appropriate. The Education Act 1993, which placed a duty on local education authorities to accept parental preference for a particular school, still leaves the final decision with that authority if they either find it would be unsuitable to their special educational needs or incompatible to the education of other children or with the use of resources (Braye and Preston-Shoot, 1997). The influence of the individual model of disability in which the disabled child is seen as being the problem and her exclusion from mainstream schooling as the solution is clear and sets boundaries around what might be achieved in changing the environment of education.

There are important implications in the continued commitment to special schools, for, as Tomlinson has shown, this is not based solely on the humanitarian ideal of providing what is best for disabled children, but also 'to cater for the needs of ordinary schools, the interests of the wider industrial society and the specific interests of professionals' (Tomlinson, 1982: 57). Indeed, in October 1997 when launching the white paper, *Excellence for all Children*, David Blunkett the Secretary of State for Education and Employment made clear his opposition to segregated education and announced his intention to reduce the numbers of children in special schools. The initial response of the National Association of School Masters and Union of Women Teachers, however, was to threaten 'not to teach' certain children if integration was to go 'too far'. It is simply unimaginable that such a threat would ever be made on the basis of gender, religion, race or virtually any other characteristic of children, but it is largely accepted as a responsible position in relation to disability. Indeed, while race and sex discrimination laws apply to education, it is specifically excluded from the provisions of the Disability Discrimination Act 1995.

It could be argued that all this is of little relevance to social work. However, it is clear that more and more parents are beginning to demand that their children be educated in ordinary schools, and in order to achieve those demands against the opposition of vested interests, talked about by Tomlinson, then parents will need help. Furthermore, the tendency of some schools to use statementing procedures as a means of permanently excluding children (ACE, 1996) runs counter to the intentions of the process to ensure inclusion. Parents and children will perhaps need advocates to intercede on their behalf and argue that it is not in the best interests of the child, either educationally or socially, that he or she be deprived of family life and links with peers and community for substantial periods during the formative years. Social workers may be ideally placed by virtue of regular contact since the birth of the disabled child to help families negotiate with the education authorities, though at present it seems that they are reluctant to take on this advocacy role and to challenge decisions made by their local authority colleagues.

What is clear is that in the future, with or without help, increasing numbers of parents will demand the social rights to an ordinary education for their children, for it is clear that for many impaired children segregated education adds educational and social disability to existing disadvantages.

Employment

The Disabled Persons (Employment) Act 1944, which has recently been substantially repealed by part II of the Disability Discrimination Act 1995, laid a framework for the provision of a variety of employment rehabilitation and resettlement services. Alongside the numerous day-centres and Adult Training Centres run by social services and health authorities, the Department of Employment operated up to 27 rehabilitation centres at their peak in the 1980s. The Department of Employment was subjected to the same market-type reforms as were the health and social services leading to its reorganisation in 1990 along the lines of a purchaser–provider split. This signalled a move away from the operation of rehabilitation services to contracting individual courses for disabled people. It was justified economically in terms of the under-use of these centres – by the time that Ingol, one of the only two regional residential Employment Resettlement Centres, closed at the end of 1991 the numbers using it had fallen into single figures – and by the changing aspirations of disabled people:

> People with disabilities increasingly insist on their right to
> be treated as individual people, not categorised; to be served
> and not managed by services; not to be unnecessarily seg-
> regated in training and work from their non-disabled col-
> leagues; to have their full potential and its development
> fairly recognised by employers and public services. (Employ-
> ment Department Group, 1990:4)

The 1944 Act also gave disabled people legal rights to
employment, in that it placed an obligation on all employers
with more than 20 workers to employ a quota of 3 per cent
of the workforce who were registered as disabled, but in practice
this was never enforced and disabled people have experienced
a higher level of unemployment than non-disabled people.
Those that do find employment are often in less skilled jobs
earning lower wages than their non-disabled counterparts.

Grover and Gladstone (1982:1) reported that 'in 1965 the
general unemployment rate was well below 2 per cent but
among registered disabled people, over 7 per cent'. By 1982
the general rate was 'something over 12 per cent while among
registered disabled people it is nearly 16 per cent'. By 1989
both the gap and the actual position of disabled people had
worsened with the figures being 5.4 per cent and 20.5 per
cent respectively (Barnes, 1991). Clearly the opportunities for
disabled people are limited but this is made worse by the
tendency of employment policies and assistance to find work
to be directed at people who are economically active, that is
actively seeking work. This works against disabled people who
may have withdrawn from what they have experienced as a
futile task. Barnes (1991) reports that the 1986 OPCS disability surveys revealed that 85 per cent of the men and 65 per
cent of the women who were not looking for work and who
defined themselves as 'unable to work' had previously taken
steps to find work but given up.

The Disability Discrimination Act 1995 replaced the quota
system and registration of disabled people in favour of defining lawful and unlawful discrimination in employment. There
are two ways in which employers would be acting unlawfully:
first, if they treat a disabled person less favourably than a
non-disabled person and cannot show that this is justified;

and, second, if they fail to provide reasonable adjustments to the working environment. Lawful discrimination results from the definitions of what might be justified in terms of treatment of a disabled person and what would be unreasonable in terms of adjustments to the environment. Justification is a complex issue and is likely to be settled through the Code of Practice issued by the Secretary of State and through case law – Gooding (1996) provides a useful and comprehensive guide to how the Act might be interpreted based on comparable experience in the USA. Certainly one aspect of such a justification would be first to show that no reasonable adjustment could be made. Here section 6(3) of the Act provides an illustrative list of what might be considered reasonable:

(a) making adjustments to premises;
(b) allocating some of the disabled person's duties to another person;
(c) transferring him to fill an existing vacancy;
(d) altering his working hours;
(e) assigning him to a different place of work;
(f) allowing him to be absent during working hours for rehabilitation, assessment or treatment;
(g) giving him, or arranging for him to be given, training;
(h) acquiring or modifying equipment;
(i) modifying instructions or reference manuals;
(j) modifying procedures for testing or assessment;
(k) providing a reader or interpreter;
(l) providing supervision.

However, as Gooding (1996:21) points out, 'an employer will not necessarily be expected to take any of these steps. He or she will be obliged to take only such steps as are reasonable in all the circumstances', and section 6(4) of the Act provides a further list of five factors that would have to be considered in determining that:

(a) the extent to which taking the step would prevent the effect in question;
(b) the extent to which it is practicable for the employer to take the step;

(c) the financial and other costs which would be incurred by the employer in taking the step and the extent to which taking it would disrupt any of his activities;

(d) the extent of the employer's financial and other resources;

(e) the availability to the employer of financial or other assistance with respect to taking the step.

While the effectiveness of this Act remains to be seen, what is certain, as far as social work intervention is concerned, is that often the major problem that many disabled people face is that of unemployment, and again the question arises as to whether it is part of the social work task to attempt to alleviate such problems. While the formal responsibility may lie with the Disability Employment Advisers (DEAs) from local Placement Assessment and Counselling Teams (PACTs), their effectiveness can be enhanced if social workers are prepared to work in an advocacy role with disabled people. Interestingly, social workers have tended to be more critical of DEAs than they have of other professionals working in the area of special education, but have not taken their task much beyond criticism. This is perhaps unfortunate, for if unemployment is assessed as the major problem, more than criticism may be needed.

They can also advocate good practice within their own organisations which may have a tendency to view disabled people as dependent clients rather than potential employees. Most local authorities themselves were below their quota when it existed and it is therefore perfectly justified for social workers to attempt to get disabled people employed in their own departments and agencies, rather than simply seeing employment as the responsibility of the DEA. In addition there are many people in day and residential care who are capable of carrying out the administrative and organisational tasks connected with the day-to-day running of such places. For example, it hardly seems professionally justifiable or cost-effective for a local day-centre to use a retired army major who is visually impaired to pack knife blades while employing someone who is able-bodied to perform clerical and administrative duties connected with the particular day-centre concerned. Thus social workers who have unemployed disabled clients should be prepared to see finding a job as part of their task, and they should be much more imaginative and practical about how they go about it, ensuring that their own employers meet their obligations as well as criticising others who fail to do so. This is one way that social workers might contribute to the task of reducing unemployment disability among their clients.

Welfare rights

The term 'welfare rights' can be interpreted in two ways: in its broadest sense it can mean the rights of the individual to all of the services provided by the welfare state; in its narrower sense it may mean the social security benefit entitlements that individuals may have. While recognising the broad use of the term, which might encompass legal and social rights as well, in this section the term will be confined to its usage in reference to the financial benefits and entitlements of disabled people.

Simkins and Tickner (1978), in their study of the financial benefit systems for disabled people, found that no less than 55 separate welfare benefits were available to disabled people. Despite this seemingly generous provision, numerous studies have shown the clear connection between poverty and disability. For example, Townsend showed that half of the appreciably or severely disabled people in the United Kingdom were living in poverty, compared with only one-fifth of able-bodied people, and he further showed that even where disabled people were in work they were poorer than their able-bodied counterparts. He concludes:

> Not only do disabled people have lower social status. They also have lower incomes and fewer assets. Moreover, they tend to be poorer even when their social status is the same as the non-disabled . . . With increasing incapacity, proportionately more people lived in house-holds with incomes below, or only marginally above that standard. Fewer lived in households with relatively high incomes. (Townsend, 1979: 711)

This level of dependency on state benefits was confirmed by the 1986 OPCS disability surveys when 78 per cent of all disabled people and 54 per cent of those below retirement age were living in households with no wage earners (Barnes, 1991). There are a number of reasons that have been suggested for the persistence of chronic poverty among disabled people. It is sometimes argued that the level of benefits is set at too low a level, and certainly evidence produced by the Royal Commission on the Distribution of Income and Wealth which reported in 1978 indicates that despite a proliferation of benefits throughout the 1970s the relative position of disabled people as a group has not changed significantly. As was noted in Chapter 2, official estimations of poverty such as the 1986 OPCS disability surveys have failed to recognise the real additional costs of impairment which is then reflected in the level at which benefits are set.

Another reason concerns the 'take-up' of various benefits for some people may not know of their existence while others may feel that application (and certainly appeal) is a stigmatising business and refuse to claim. A final reason concerns the complexity of the system, with its overlapping benefits, different eligibility criteria and other administrative problems that often make claiming a nightmare. Despite a number of changes to the system, the difficulties of the 'welfare-benefits jungle' are still well captured by Simkins and Tickner:

> To illustrate the tangle of criteria needed to make the present system work, let us consider a person with one or both legs amputated. If he is seeking a payment under War Pensions or Industrial Injury schemes, he must first establish where and how the damage was caused, and then the size of the payment made to the amputee would depend on a schedule, in 10 per cent steps, in effect needing a reply to the question: 'how much of the limb/limbs have you lost?'
>
> For the Mobility Allowance the question would be 'are you unable or virtually unable to walk, and likely to remain so?' – the applicant who can walk a relatively short distance with the help of artificial limbs may not get the allowance even if he has no feet.
>
> If an Attendance Allowance were being sought, the ques-

tion is 'how much help do you have to have?'

For the contributory benefits the approach is 'never mind the leg, how about your payments record?'

For Supplementary Benefits, or to find out how much a home help would cost (if one is available), the question is 'how poor are you?' and for some local authority benefits, 'how isolated are you from relatives whom we might expect to help you?'

For some local authority benefits the key question may well be 'where do you live?' For a few people who lived in the wrong spot at the time of local government boundary reorganisation, entitlement vanished over-night without the applicant moving from his bed.

And of course if the amputee is a 'housewife', the authorities are not interested in her leg, only in the answer to: 'what kind of contribution record or income does your husband have?' And for the single woman: 'are you cohabiting with a man to whom you are not married?'

(Simkins and Tickner, 1978:51–2)

Given that these criticisms are valid, there seem to be three fairly simple solutions to the problems of poverty and disability: raise the level of benefits; make them available as a right and reduce the number of eligibility tests; and, finally, simplify the system. However, these are not realistic possibilities in the short term, and even where change has been forced as in the case of the European court's ruling that the additional housewife's test for Non-Contributory Invalidity Pension was discriminatory, it resulted in a tightening of criteria to the Severe Disability Allowance that replaced it in order to ensure no overall additional expenditure.

In April 1992 there was an attempt to rationalise some benefits when the Mobility and Attendance Allowances were merged into the Disability Living Allowance (DLA), though the latter remains for those over 65 years old. The mobility component is paid at two rates and the attendance component at three, resulting in 11 possible levels at which this might be paid, plus refusal. One of the aims of the introduction of the DLA was to extend the reach of these benefits to people with 'moderate' disabilities as research had showed that they fared worse than those with either 'severe' or 'mild' impairments. Within 12 months of its introduction it had overshot its target of 300 000 claimants, and by November 1994 had reached 430 000 (Burgess, 1996). However, despite this apparent success, the evaluation of the DLA carried out for the Department of Social Security also showed that less that 30 per cent of people who requested claim packs actually returned them though the researchers were unable to follow any of these up and could only speculate that it may have much to do with the pack being too long and complex for many people to complete (ibid.).

This explanation is supported by a study (Daly and Noble, 1996) which sought to examine the effectiveness of DLA by looking at a representative sample of disabled people and their take-up of this benefit, which did allow them to also examine the characteristics of people who were not in receipt of DLA. They found that 43 per cent of their sample did not receive DLA and that this did not correlate to any measure of severity of disability. They recommended in their conclusion:

> 'Don't fill in this form yourself!' was the advice of one interviewee, when asked about the 40-page DLA claim form, echoing the view of many who would emphasise the importance of the questions being rephrased and mediated by experienced users of the claim pack. (Daly and Noble, 1996:49)

In addition to the widespread problem of non-receipt of DLA, Daly and Noble found considerable variations in the rates that were paid to those in receipt which led them to conclude that 'the only confident statement to be made about benefit reach is that those who cannot walk at all, the utterly immobile, will be in receipt of mobility award, if this condition set in before their 65th birthday' (ibid.:48).

For the social worker, who has a disabled client whose poverty is current, immediate action is necessary and social workers have a record of being effective advocates when they do help their clients with benefits issues. The first approach is to make sure that the client is receiving all the entitled benefits, and in order to do that the social worker may need to resort to additional help – otherwise the myths that some professionals hold like 'you can't get the attendance component if you work', or 'you can't get the mobility component if you can walk', will continue to abound. The first place to start is with the Disability Rights Handbook, which is produced every year by the Disability Alliance with Scope and is the simplest yet most accurate and comprehensive guide to welfare benefits and it is a guide that both social workers and their disabled clients can use. This will also keep social workers up to date with the tribunal and court rulings that may have a relevance for disabled people who have previously had claims rejected. If more expert advice is needed then the Disablement Income Group (DIG), the Disability Alliance or other local organisations like Disablement Information and Advice Line (DIAL) may be able to help, not just with information but also possibly with representation at appeals or tribunals. In short, in order to minimise poverty and reduce economic disability, it is important that disabled people receive all the benefits to which they are entitled.

A second approach is to set up a disability rights project where a number of disabled people in a particular area or day-centre are assessed by welfare rights experts to see whether they are getting all that they are entitled to. The most spectacularly successful such project was undertaken in Strathclyde (Casserly and Clark, 1978), where 72 disabled people attending a day-centre were assessed as to their entitlements. Only six were receiving their full entitlement and a further 50 had their benefits increased, on average by £6.10 a week (1977 figures), and overall the group's income was increased by over £15 000 per annum. Other similar projects throughout Britain have also substantially increased benefits for disabled people and it is worth considering the establishment of similar projects elsewhere.

Since 1993, with the transfer of some of the Income Support functions and the Independent Living Fund to local authorities, social workers themselves have taken on a much greater role in income maintenance. With the Community Care (Direct Payments) Act 1996, this role will grow and it is essential that as well as advocating for and assisting disabled people with benefits provided through the Benefits Agency, social workers are going to have to work within their own organisations. Depending on the level to which budgets have been devolved, this may mean challenging the decisions of managers or having their own decisions challenged by others. The basis on which social workers either challenge decisions or respond to such challenges is a matter of professional practice as much as it is procedural, as this area of payments is one that is directly related to an assessment of need rather than rights-based eligibility criteria.

A similar situation applies to district council improvement grants and Disabled Facilities Grants which, because they are outside the main Benefits Agency system, do not have the clear review and appeals procedures of other benefits. There is evidence (Sapey, 1995) that this leads to officials exercising their judgements in a subjective manner which requires different skills to challenge than with the rule-bound decisions of an adjudication officer.

A longer-term solution involves working with established disability organisations towards the eventual provision of a national disability income as of right. Both DIG and the Disability Alliance have put forward proposals for such a scheme, and while both organisations would argue that their proposals are radically different, to the outsider they look broadly similar. Part of the conflict may stem from the fact that the Alliance is part of the 'poverty lobby' and thus to the left politically, whereas DIG is avowedly non-political.

Not all organisations are united in this 'incomes approach' to disability. The Union of the Physically Impaired Against Segregation suggested that poverty was a symptom of disabled people's oppression and not the cause, and consequently it may be inappropriate to attack the symptom without dealing with the cause. UPIAS advanced three fundamental principles:

disability is a social situation, caused by social conditions, which requires for its elimination

(a) that no one aspect such as incomes, mobility, or institutions is treated in isolation,

(b) that disabled people should, with the help and advice of others, assume control over their own lives, and

(c) that professionals, experts and others who seek to help must be committed to promoting such control by disabled people.

(UPIAS, 1976:3)

It could be argued that financial benefits fall within the province of the Benefits Agency and that therefore social workers should not get involved. However, there are two arguments that can counter this: it is clear that the Benefits Agency cannot be relied on to ensure that disabled people get their entitlements; and as poverty is a major problem for many disabled people, it is an abrogation of professional responsibility not to make any attempt to alleviate it. Both individual welfare rights advice, provided it is accurate, and the establishment of welfare rights projects are thus part of the social work task. Involvement in the incomes approach to disability, however, can be viewed as a personal rather than professional responsibility, and while social workers may join organisations in their spare time active involvement in the politics of disability might be considered beyond their professional duty. The difficulty with this position however is that it involves sitting on the fence which has the effect of supporting the *status quo*, which in turn implies support for the continuation of policies that leave disabled people in poverty.

The rights of disabled people: ways forward?

It is clear then that disabled people do currently have certain limited rights not to be discriminated against in the employment market, to education commensurate with need, and to a whole range of benefits and services. However, it is plain that many disabled people do not get these rights and there are raging arguments about how best the rights of disabled people should be safeguarded and extended. These arguments have been characterised as 'persuasion versus enforcement' or 'the carrot versus the stick' (Oliver, M., 1982). The persuasionist view suggests that discrimination against disabled people arises as the result of either negative attitudes or the failure to consider particular 'special' needs. From this point of view what is needed is more information, public education campaigns and research.

The enforcement view, on the other hand, suggests that strong legal action is necessary, for it is only then that disabled people will achieve their rights. There are three problems with this view, however:

(a) Even if legislation is passed, it may not be enforced – the Disabled Persons (Employment) Act 1944 is a good example of this.

(b) Even if legislation is passed and enforced, it may not achieve its aim of ending discrimination. Both the Equal Pay and Race Relations Acts are examples of this.

(c) Such legislation tends to operate to the benefit of certain sections of the professional classes rather than serve to protect the interests of all the groups for whom the legislation was designed.

(Oliver, M., 1982:78)

Thus, it has been suggested by Shearer (1981b) that what is needed is some additional anti-discrimination legislation. This call for anti-discrimination legislation has been picked up by a number of disabled people and their organisations, and since 1982 there have been 13 unsuccessful attempts to get such an enactment through parliament (Barnes and Oliver, 1995). After the last attempt, the Civil Rights (Disabled Persons) Bill was defeated in 1994 with the connivance of the Minister for Disabled People and the government was effectively forced to introduce their own bill which has now become the Disability Discrimination Act 1995. It does not, however, meet the aspirations of the disabled people's movement, partially because it bases its understanding of disability on an individual, rather than a social model, but also because it appears to be intended to be ineffective. Gooding summarises the problems:

The Disability Discrimination Act 1995 is indeed a confusing, contorted and unsatisfactory piece of legislation. It signally fails to establish the clear principle of equal treatment which should be the essence of a law countering discrimination. (It has, for example, three separate definitions of what constitutes discrimination applying in different sections). The Act's fatal equivocation towards the principle of equality for disabled people has produced an extremely complicated and unclear law, hedged around with exceptions and justifications. Lord Lester, the prominent civil liberties lawyer, described it as 'riddled with vague, slippery and elusive exceptions making it so full of holes that it was more like a colander than a binding code' [Hansard, 22 May 1995, 813].

The Act's exclusion of crucial areas of social life, such as education and small businesses, makes no logical sense, and can be understood only as the product of inter-Cabinet compromises, and a concern to control potential Treasury Costs.

Above all, the Act's lack of any effective enforcement mechanism undermines any claim to be a sincere attempt at ending a social evil. This crucial weakness, combined with the vagueness of certain key concepts and the absence of a timetable for the full implementation of the Act's provisions, makes it impossible to predict the actual impact of this potentially far-reaching new law.   (Gooding, 1996:1)

The incoming Labour government of 1997 announced at their party's annual conference that year that they would act in respect of two of these criticisms, namely ensuring the early implementation of part III of the Act and in setting up a Disability Rights Commission to ensure its effectiveness. The British Council of Disabled People (BCODP) reacted to this by calling for the 1995 Act to be repealed and replaced with legislation set in a social, not medical framework. Their view of the commission promised by the Labour government was that it would simply be policing a bad piece of legislation rather than protecting and enforcing the rights of disabled people.

The development of BCODP and of similar organisations in other countries over the past few decades, including the formation of Disabled People's International, represents an important challenge to the dominance of the individual model of disability. In the disabled people's movement individuals have been able to assert their own positive self-identity, organise collectively in political campaigns, develop arts and literature that reflect the experience of disability, and to refine the analysis of disability that challenges quite fundamentally the way we all see ourselves. It is from this growing consciousness and political power of disabled people that ultimately solutions to the problems of disability may emerge.

In conclusion, it may be difficult for social workers as professionals to participate fully in the growing political movement of disabled people, though there may be scope for working with these emergent organisations. However, this will have implications for the 'professional attitude' to professional practice in general and disabled people in particular, and it is a theme which will be considered further in the final chapter. Clearly, however, there are a number of important social work tasks to be tackled in a society not totally committed to the ultimate goal of removing the disabling consequences of impairment.

7

Conclusions: Some Professional and Organisational Aspects of Social Work with Disabled People

This final chapter will attempt to bring together some of the issues thrown up by attempting to apply the social model of disability to social work as an organised professional activity. It will begin by looking at some of the conclusions and recommendations that were made in the first edition of this book 15 years ago, in 1983, and will then consider what progress if any has been made and what now needs to be done.

Some professional concerns in 1983

The main professional problem was that in trying to develop an adequate conceptualisation of social work in this area, there were few, if any, existing models or frameworks adequate for the purpose. While both the Central Council for Education and Training in Social Work (CCETSW) and the British Association of Social Workers (BASW) had made attempts to define the roles and tasks of social workers with disabled people and to recommend levels of training that were needed (CCETSW, 1974; BASW, 1982), they proved inadequate for a number of reasons and two in particular.

The first of these was that both organisations were developing their guidance from an individual model of disability which led them to assume a causal relationship between impairment and disability. This was clearly inappropriate from a social model analysis, as someone with a very severe impairment may only be mildly disabled whereas someone with a minor impairment may be totally disabled by poverty, poor housing, the attitudes of employers or hostile social treatment. A scarce resource like professional expertise should be allocated on the extent of disability, not on the extent of impairment.

The second reason was that neither of these two attempts to lay a professional basis for the practice of social work with disabled people really came to grips with the perennial problem of the relationship between theory and practice, and the individual and social models of disability are dependent upon that relationship, either overtly or covertly. Thus it could be said that the individual model stems from the 'personal tragedy theory of disability', whereas the social model stems from 'the social problem theory of disability'.

An attempt to look at this problem in the context of social work generally was made by Lee (in Bailey and Lee, 1982:16), who distinguished between three levels:

Level 1   *Actual task*
Level 2   *Technical knowledge*
Level 3   *Theoretical knowledge*

While, ideally, good social work practice should be based upon an integration of all three levels, in reality there is often a polarisation between 'academics' and 'practitioners', with each group seeing its sphere of activity as unrelated to the other. Lee, however, suggests that 'speculative theory with scant regard for practice (level 1) is of little utility, and practice insulated from theoretical questions (level 3) while perfectly permissible in car maintenance, is downright dangerous in social work' (in Bailey and Lee, 1982:17).

The problem with both the CCETSW and BASW attempts to establish a framework was that they had almost totally been concerned with the relationship between levels 1 and 2, whereas the social model of disability is concerned primarily with the relationship between levels 2 and 3. There were a number of reasons for this. Articulated theories about disability were few and far between, as were considerations of their relationship to technical knowledge. Also, it is extremely difficult to draw up a skills manual for social workers as one might for plumbers, electricians or car mechanics. Finally, much work with disabled people has been atheoretical, either based covertly upon the individual model of disability, or simply orientated to the immediate practical task at hand. This approach has problems, for, as Lee has argued:

> theory must have regard for practice but it should not be 'tailored' for it. Practical contingencies must not be allowed to dictate the terms of theoretical speculation, for if they do a most anaemic form of theorising will result. Such theory, raised in a protected environment to fit necessity, is the stuff of car maintenance manuals; and people informed by such manuals might be able to perform reasonably efficiently, but then so could unreflexive automatons. (in Bailey and Lee, 1982:41)

While the social model of disability would provide an adequate and appropriate base for developing social work practice with disabled people, much social work was and is inherently conservative and does not challenge existing social relations. Deeply embedded as it is in social consciousness generally, the individual model or personal disaster theory of disability can only be replaced or superseded by a radical change in both theoretical conceptualisation and practical approach. This had fundamental implications both for the training needs of social workers and for the professional organisation of generic social work. It was, and is, not enough merely to increase knowledge about disability on basic training courses; this must be tackled alongside a reversion towards specialist practice and away from the generic approach.

One of the main barriers to the development of a radical approach to social work with disabled people was the low status attached to such work. The problems of both organisational orientation and professional commitment to work with disabled people were rooted in the post-Seebohm creation of social services departments. Satyamurti described the experience in the department she studied:

As the time of reorganisation drew nearer, CCOs [child care officers] began to feel more anxiety at the prospect of it. Many of them felt distaste at the idea of working with elderly and physically handicapped people, or were worried about having to deal with the mentally ill. Others felt not so much distaste as a sense that their professional status would be eroded by having to do 'welfare-type' work. As one qualified CCO put it, 'I didn't do social work training in order to sit and have friendly chats with lonely old ladies.' Many were concerned at the possibility of being overwhelmed by the huge caseloads coming from the Welfare Department and were pessimistic about maintaining standards of work. Welfare Department social workers, for their part, discerned that both they and their clients were despised by the Children's Department, and felt that they would be subordinated in the new department to a 'child care' way of doing things. For both groups, part of the anxiety centred on the question of who would get the senior and management positions in the new department – from which former disciplines would they be drawn? (Satyamurti, 1981:20)

It was clear that child care was given priority, but this is not solely due to the fact that it was, on the whole, former child-care specialists who achieved most of the managerial positions in the new departments. There were other organisational pressures which trapped social workers as well as their clients in particular forms of social relations engendered by welfare bureaucracies.

Some organisational concerns in 1983

The organisational concerns were threefold: first that social workers act as arbiters of need between disabled people and the state; second, that the responsibilities for services to disabled people were uncoordinated and distributed between a large number of organisations and rehabilitation professions; and, finally, the services that were available tended to reflect the professional interests and aspirations of those workers rather than being based on any analysis of disability and the needs of disabled people.

The issue of the relationship between the needs of disabled people and the services provided is a complicated one in which there is no direct link between the two. The complexities of the relationship can best be illustrated by means of a diagram (such as Figure 7.1). From this diagram it is clear that there is no direct relationship between the needs of disabled people and the services they receive. Rather, disabled people had their needs defined and interpreted by others, and the services provided to meet these needs were often delivered by large, bureaucratic organisations. Where the crucial problem was to ration scarce resources among competing demands, social workers and social work training was not necessarily the most suited to this particular role, and other organisational pressures often led to the exclusion of a professional approach to this task.

The experiences of social workers when working for the Family Fund were, in microcosm, the experiences of many social workers in social services departments. Bradshaw describes some of the dilemmas:

> the discretion of the social worker in the Fund's offices in York began to be constrained by pressure of work and the Panel's decisions. The rising number of applications and cases pending soon made it very difficult for social workers to spend the time needed to carry out the detailed inquiries upon which their discretion had to be used. Alarmed by the backlog, the Fund's managers began to introduce routine procedures and to urge social workers to reduce the time spent on each case. Routine cases were given to unqualified staff and all were urged to confine themselves to the item requested and not 'try to do casework at a distance'. The social workers, feeling that the problem arose as a result of delays in recruiting staff, were unwilling to accept limits imposed on their professional judgment, and they were not happy in seeing needs that they had recognised go unmet because they did not have the time to intervene. The tensions arising from these restraints on the exercise of professional discretion and the need to speed up the making of grants continued throughout the phase of exploratory development; they were heightened further by the body of rules that began to emerge from the Panel about

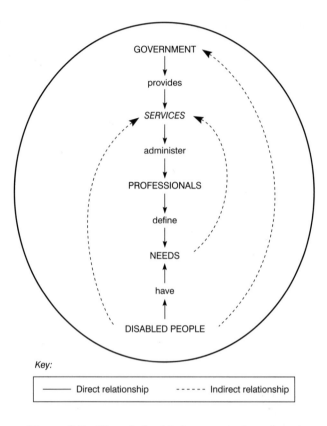

Figure 7.1 *The relationship between needs and services*

Source: Oliver, M. (1982:57).

what kind of help could be given, and from the Medical Advisory Panel about which children were eligible. (Bradshaw, 1980:41)

As a consequence of this social workers tended to leave the Fund and were gradually replaced by administrators. The problem for social workers in social services departments, however, was not merely one of lack of opportunities to work in different ways elsewhere, but was also exacerbated by the failure of the profession to distinguish between professional and administrative criteria for decision-making, and further to support workers who wished to make decisions based on the former rather than the latter.

However, Figure 7.1 is in itself simplistic and two additional aspects are important: first, the overlapping organisational context in which services are delivered; and, second, the people who deliver the services.

Blaxter (1980) found that services for disabled people could be provided by more than a dozen different organisations. These tended to be large, bureaucratic and remote, and consequently they found it difficult to respond to individual needs in a personalised way. Furthermore, there was considerable overlap as to the services provided, and demarcation lines were often blurred. As a consequence disabled people were passed from one department to another, or asked the same questions many times and this did little to enhance their quality of life.

Because of these complexities and overlapping services it was often suggested that 'coordination' is a major problem in providing services for disabled people. However, the real problem was not coordination but, as Wilding says, the consequences of services which had been built up around professional skills rather than client need:

> Services organised around professional skills are a tribute to the power of professionals in policy making. They also bear witness to a failure of professional responsibility. This is a failure to recognise that services organised around particular skills may be logical for professionals but may not meet the needs of clients and potential clients. *The real sufferers, for example, from the multiplicity of professionals actually or potentially involved in the care and rehabilitation of the physically handicapped are the handicapped.* (Wilding, 1982:98, our emphasis)

Finkelstein also suggested that the problem was not one of coordination but one of the need for a change in professional role – the professional must change from expert definer of need and/or rationer of services, and become a resource which the disabled person might use as he or she chooses:

The endemic squabbles between rehabilitation workers about professional boundaries and the familiar farce of professional 'teamwork' can only be put at an end when all the workers and facilities in rehabilitation become resources in a process of self-controlled rehabilitation. (Finkelstein, 1981:27)

For social workers in local authority social services departments, however, the problems were not only those of a service organised around narrow professional skills or even lack of coordination and teamwork, but also of working in departments where there was little or no recognition of the exercise of professional skills in working with disabled people. It could be argued that Seebohm did not create generic departments but specialist childcare ones, where the needs of children were met by trained professionals and other needs and obligations were met by unqualified staff, welfare assistants and the like, or passed on to the ever-growing number of occupational therapists being employed by SSDs.

Despite this low priority, a disabled person could be confronted with more than a dozen different professionals from health and social welfare agencies. A major problem for disabled people and their families, therefore, was not just a matter of which particular agency to approach but also of which particular professional to contact. Furthermore, even when professionals were in contact, disabled people and their families are often unclear which department the professional represents and consequently what services may, or may not, be offered. To overcome this the idea of a *'named person'* was gradually being built into practice.

However, there were a number of problems related to the idea, particularly about whether the named person would in fact be the 'key worker' or simply someone given nominal responsibility, like the head of a special school. There was also the question about whether most professionals had sufficient knowledge and skills to act in this capacity, and both in terms of their strategic position and Finkelstein's principle of self-controlled rehabilitation the disabled person was the most logical choice as both named person and key-worker. The professional task, therefore, should not have been to usurp the key-worker position from the disabled person, but rather work with him or her to ensure that the required knowledge was acquired and thereby allay fears that a new profession of 'named persons' would arise with its own career structure, salary increments and enhanced professional status.

There were a number of other problems to which the professional relationship could give rise. McKnight (1981) had suggested that the very relationship was itself disabling, and others (Robinson, 1978; Fox, 1974) had pointed to the fact that very often professional definitions of need did not coincide with needs defined by disabled people themselves. Consequently where professional and personal definitions of need conflicted, the quality of life for disabled people was unlikely to be enhanced. Scott, who had written perceptively on the topic, stated that the professional

> has been specially trained to give professional help to impaired people. He cannot use his expertise if those who are sent to him for assistance do not regard themselves as being impaired. Given this fact, it is not surprising that the doctrine has emerged among experts that truly effective rehabilitation and adjustment can occur only after the client has squarely faced and accepted the 'fact' that he is, indeed, 'impaired'. (Scott, 1970:280)

And it was not just in terms of 'acceptance of disability' but also in the assessment of needs and services that professionals sought to impose their definitions, though not always with total success. Thus many disabled people had their needs met (or not) by professionalised welfare bureaucracies which very often did not provide the appropriate service in an acceptable fashion. While this might have implied that the welfare state had to be dismantled to make progress, there were a few less drastic solutions.

Some ways forward in 1983

This analysis of disability and of the social work task with disabled people resulted in five main recommendations for change: the first involved a recognition of the right of individuals to take responsibility for their own health and lifestyle; second, that participation within the provision of services and within the social work/client relationship was essential to changing the unequal power relations that exist in welfare; third, that political organisation of disabled people needed to develop in order to challenge the intransigence of those in positions of power; fourth, that a mutual sharing of responsibility between disabled people and professionals was essential and that organisational barriers to such practice needed to be removed; and, finally, that while this analysis results in a focus on material resources this should not be taken as a denial of the value or importance of emotional support.

While the role of individuals in taking responsibility for their own health and welfare had been widely accepted and promoted, the Chronically Sick and Disabled Persons Act had been criticised for taking away from the individual responsibility for his or her own life-style:

> The goodwill behind the 1970 Act's provision cannot be doubted. But the philosophy can, for what it does is to reinforce the notion that people who happen to have disabilities are people who are 'helpless', unable to choose for themselves the aid to opportunity they need. What this effectively does is to lock them into service providers' perception of what is good for them, and so limit rather than expand their areas of effective choice. (Shearer, 1981b:82)

Shearer's solution to this problem was to provide more cash rather than services, but she asserted that this by itself would not be enough and that such provision must be reinforced by anti-discrimination legislation to guarantee disabled people the right to participate fully in all aspects of their lives.

There were two areas in which participation could be important. To begin with, disabled people could participate in the provision of services, but few local authorities were prepared to employ disabled workers. The other level of participation is in the professional/client relationship, though whether this should be on an equal basis or whether the disabled person should be the master and the professional the servant was a matter of some debate. There had been a variety of calls for providing adequate training to help professionals develop new forms of practice to meet changing needs, including the CCETSW report (1974), the Jay Report (1979) and the Royal Commission on the National Health Service (1979). Disabled people, too, were specifying the directions in which practice must move:

> The basis of professional practice must rest on an assumption of integration and a commitment to promoting control by disabled people over their own lives. Since the lives of disabled people also depend on the actions of helpers, control over education, training and role of such helpers needs to be vested in disabled people (quite aside from the need for more disabled people to enter the profession).
>
> What this means in practice is that the role of the professional worker in rehabilitation, for example, needs to change from management of the patient to that of being a resource for the patient to use in reaching his or her own goals. The suggestion that professional workers in rehabilitation should become a resource to be utilised by disabled people is not a suggestion that professionals should become passive and all the onus for innovation, assessment, decision making, etc. should fall on the shoulders of disabled people. Professionals acting as a resource to be used by others need special education and training so that they are able to promote control by disabled people. (Finkelstein, 1981:26)

Partly as a response to this lack of participation, many disabled people had begun to investigate and develop alternative possibilities and a number of these were concerned in the area of self-help and health (Robinson and Henry, 1977). Furthermore, disabled people and their organisations were not just restricting their activities to health, but were also extending them to the social consequences of disability and banding together in order to gain access to much needed support services.

This growing number of organisations of and for disabled people could be classified in terms of one of four particular approaches: the partnership approach; the income approach; the self-help approach and; the populist approach (Oliver, M.,

1982). The partnership approach developed first and there are a large number of voluntary organisations which provide services for disabled people similar to the ones provided by statutory agencies, though usually care is taken not to duplicate provision – hence the partnership. In the late 1960s and early 1970s two other types of group began to spring up. First, there were groups concerned to tackle the issue of poverty and disability – hence the income approach. Second, and partly as a consequence of the failure of the partnership approach and organisations for disabled people to meet the needs of disabled people as they themselves defined them, self-help and populist approaches developed.

The crucial difference between these two approaches is that self-help groups have tended to organise around particular clinical conditions or problems, while populist groups have taken particular clinical conditions or problems for granted and have been much more concerned to set up democratic organisations controlled by their membership. It was largely groups who were organising on a self-help or populist basis who were calling for more participation, changed professional practice and ultimately the removal of the disabling aspects of impairment.

One crucial dimension that had recently emerged in disability organisations was the distinction between organisations *of* disabled people and organisations for disabled people. According to one commentator:

> Organisations for the disabled outnumber organisations of disabled people by 100 to 1 and disabled people are missing from the governing bodies of the former and from their workforce. Moreover, organisations for the disabled, which proudly represent the interests of disabled people to government – and are used and supported by government for this purpose – often lack direct contact with disabled people, and are often very inadequately accountable to them. (Large, 1981:6)

Organisations of disabled people were becoming an increasingly potent force and consequently professionals, including social workers, would need to build links with such organisations

and develop the skills necessary to work in ways radically different from those needed with organisations following the partnership approach.

Very often the response of professionals when confronted
with patients or clients who asserted the right to control their
own bodies or social circumstances was to doubt their capacity
to cope and also to feel vaguely threatened by such self-
assertiveness. However, there were two positive aspects to this.
To begin with, many disabled people were more aware than
anyone else of their physical conditions and the social consequences of them simply as a result of experiencing them
every single day of their lives. And, further, the taking of responsibility by patients or clients removed, or at least decreased,
the burden of responsibility upon the professional.

No doubt in many professional/client interactions mutual
sharing of responsibility took place. However, the first crucial
task of the 1980s ought to have been to create organisational
structures which facilitated this shift in responsibility so that
services would be flexibly geared to the needs of the disabled
person. And the second crucial task should have been to alter
professional practice so that it was the disabled person who
was in control and not the social worker or another professional.
Social work practice with disabled people needed to move in
these directions if it was not to be inadequate, unsatisfactory,
uninspired and ultimately demeaning both for the social worker
and the disabled person.

Finally, three of the essential social work tasks identified in
the Barclay Report – social care planning, community social work
and counselling – were the three most important tasks identified by this analysis. Not only that, but following the social
model of disability this book placed emphasis upon material
resources while not denying the importance of emotional support. The Barclay Report came to similar conclusions:

> The emphasis by physically handicapped people was very
> much on material help. But they recognised the need for
> support and help in coming to terms with handicap and
> for families in coping with the emotional stresses and ten-
> sions within marriages to which dependence or handicap
> may give rise. (Barclay Committee, 1982:163)

ndations provided a framework against which
e effective services for and with disabled people,
ιe possibility of making the relationships between
ιple and social workers more effective and fruitful
ιerned than they had been up to then. Just how
changed in 15 years and what now needs to be
done ⌐ ιhat is considered next.

Theoretical and professional developments

The articulation of disability from a theoretical viewpoint has increased dramatically over the last couple of decades resulting in the establishment of disability studies as a subject of study within universities in Britain and the USA. Within this growing literature a number of writers have begun to propose how such ideas can be translated into the technical knowledge and skills that are required to practice social work. As the earlier chapters have indicated, some of these writers are from within the social work profession while others are activists within the disabled people's movement, but what is perhaps of importance here is the extent to which either of these groups have managed to influence the institutions of the social work profession.

In relation to the social work task, both BASW and CCETSW have made some attempt to recognise, at least in terms of official policy, that disability arises as a consequence of social forces, but neither have responded fully to the need to develop a practice that is informed by such theorising. In the case of BASW, while their 1990 AGM unanimously passed a motion recognising that disability resulted from the social reactions to impairment, their policy documents continued to reflect an individual-model understanding of the problem. In a discussion document on the subject (BASW, 1990) they describe the nature of disability as initially caused by impairment, but that the impact of this on individuals and families depends on severity; prognosis; origin; social barriers; age; social impact; changes in personal functioning; and changes in social functioning. This paper goes on to describe the social work role in terms of a series of functional tasks including taking responsibility for 'whether the disabled person can appreciate danger and act accordingly', clearly viewing independent living as potentially at odds with a societal responsibility to protect 'vulnerable' individuals. This description is little more than a reiteration of what is happening within an individual model of practice, leaving the recommendations clearly at the technical knowledge/actual task levels.

The problem with this conceptualisation is the same as with the Disability Discrimination Act in that while discrimination against disabled people is recognised, much of it is considered reasonable given their understanding that disability results from impairment. The systematic exclusion of people with impairments is not acknowledged and hence a welfare response to individual inadequacies remains a plausible solution. However, the document does endorse the view that in managing care services, the first assumption should be that disabled people will wish to do this for themselves and that they are the most appropriate people to do so. While this is to be welcomed, until it is within the context of viewing disability from a social model it is unlikely to achieve much more than participation within a functional service to impairment.

Following the launch of the Diploma in Social Work in 1989, CCETSW formed a number of working parties to develop detailed performance criteria for social work students in a range of areas of particular practice. Their report *Disability Issues: Developing Anti-discriminatory Practice* (Stevens, 1991) clearly recommends that disability should be viewed in terms of the social model, but CCETSW were simultaneously immersed in the development of a competence-based vocational qualification, in which theory is only selected if it is critical to enabling practice. Avoiding the dangers of an 'anaemic form of theorising' (Bailey and Lee, 1982), little was stated by Stevens about the social work task and instead his report concentrated on the issue of participation by producing guidelines for the training of disabled people as social workers.

However, with CCETSW providing uncritical support to the government's quest for vocational qualifications, the actual content of that training has followed a competence approach based upon a functional analysis of social work activity within local authority agencies, which has itself been dominated by an individual model of disability. The result once again is a failure to get to grips with the perennial problem of the relationship between theory and practice, and some argue that CCETSW may have rejected this relationship as irrelevant to social work practice (Jones, 1994).

The paradox is that CCETSW has placed a considerable importance on such values as empowerment, participation and choice in welfare and has taken a lead in this respect through the development of anti-discriminatory practice in the social work curriculum. The foundation of such practice is that the social problems which individuals, families and communities face are often the result of systematic oppression within the structures of British society. At the same time it has adopted a competence model of education which according to some has left social work:

> foundering in the mechanistic application of a political correctness which represents an ill-digested, prescriptive and rule-bound approach to which students must submit or rebel, but which they have little scope to interrogate and own, and the original point of which may well elude them. (Froggett and Sapey 1997:50)

While part of the explanation for this paradox is the pressure brought to bear on the organisation by the government, it may also be due to the nature of social work values. Holman argues that the ideology that underpins BASW's *Code of Ethics for Social Work* is in fact intensely individualistic, and that while it may be correct to uphold the valuing of individuals:

> a focus which minimizes considerations of mutual obligations, of environment and structures, contains certain drawbacks. For a start it opens the door to explanations of human problems which stress the inadequacy of individuals regardless of their circumstances. This individualism has something in common with that of the New Right and its conception of an underclass of feckless individuals to be condemned and controlled. Then it diminishes the resolve to campaign against poverty and other societal forces, for they are regarded as outside the real scope of social work,

which is just to deal with individuals. Not least, the climate that social work is to do with a professional coping with an individual client is a barrier to social workers acting collectively with user organizations and residents of communities. (Holman, 1993:51–2)

For Holman the solution lies in the development of mutuality as the basis of the relationship between the state, and hence social workers as administrators of its welfare functions, and the recipients of welfare. Mutuality is a development of the socialist value of fraternity and a social work practice that was underpinned by this might be capable of responding to the criticisms of the social-model analysis. Not only would it imply a mutual sharing of responsibility with disabled people and that the social work role was one of supporting individuals to achieve their own aspirations, it would also mean that for social workers to be truly effective in helping people to be less disabled they would have to view the struggle of the disabled people's movement as directly affecting them also. The model of social work that would follow from this ideology would be based upon the notion that a world in which particular groups of people are systematically oppressed is oppressive to all people.

The individual model of disability and its associated themes of deviancy and normality are very much the product of the modernist project and its search for scientific certainty, yet still influenced by the traditional need for strong social hierarchies. In such a world people are identified and develop an identity as normal or abnormal, and the social model helps us to understand how this has becomes a systematic process of oppression. In the struggle against oppression the oppressed will challenge the identity bestowed upon them, but what is also required is a similar challenge from the oppressors. Stuart Hall argues in relation to race that this may be happening:

with globalisation comes the growing recognition that nobody has one identity. There isn't anyone who doesn't have complex cultural roots. The Brits suddenly discover half of them are really French, they speak a language partly based on Norse, they came from Scandinavia, they're Romans, many have gone to live in Australia and the Himalayas. (quoted in Jaques, 1997:34)

The result of this is to break down some of the notions that underpin racism, and in particular the ideology of superiority that permits white people to justify their oppression of black people. What would be required in relation to disability is for non-disabled people to discover that they may be as different from the ideal human body as those that they had considered as impaired, and as such are not part of a distinct and superior group. Hall (ibid.:35) suggests that 'we are living in a period not simply of homogenisation but of homogeneity *and* difference', in other words we occupy one world in which difference is increasingly valued rather than being seen as a cause for fear. In this world, even if the acts of oppression are not directly aimed at non-disabled people, their world is made worse because of its existence.

Thus, to professionalise social work on the basis of an expertise in impairment as a cause of social need would be an act of oppression as this would serve to reinforce theories of individual inadequacy and blame, whereas what is required is for social workers and social work to develop a commitment to the removal of disabling barriers in partnership with disabled people.

It is therefore not simply a matter of whether to have specialist or generic forms of social work training and practice, or of the subordination of welfare work with disabled people to the priorities of child protection, but there remains the need for a fundamental shift towards a radical rather than individualistic practice. Neither are the problems of disabled people or of social workers resolved by the incorporation of empowerment as an instrumental competence within the curriculum. In part this is because of the anti-theoretical approach of competence-based education, but primarily it is because this actually represents part of the process of disempowering disabled people by providing bureaucratic measures to limit the effectiveness of protest and self-empowerment.

Organisational issues and structural developments

Fifteen years ago this book was concerned that with an increasingly functional view of needs and their assessment, social work was being considered as an unsuitable training for what was becoming a proceduralised activity of rationing resources. Furthermore, the response to uncoordinated services was one of appointing 'named persons' and there was a danger that this might develop into yet another profession within an individual model of disability. Since then the procedural approach has received official sanction through the National Health Service and Community Care Act 1990 which, by introducing quasi-markets, also placed budget control at the top of local authority priorities. Care managers were appointed from April 1993, since when the range of books on care management from within the social work profession already outnumber those that have been written about social work with disabled people, and the first courses in this new occupation have begun to appear. And yet, despite this pessimistic assessment, the Community Care (Direct Payments) Act 1996 holds out the potential for the most fundamental reorganisation of welfare for half a century.

The Seebohm reorganisation of welfare was one that focused on the organisation of the institutions through which social work was delivered without challenging the basic principles of welfare that had been laid down in 1948, and as such the progression or regression that followed can be accounted for in terms of changing bureaucratic mechanisms. However, the changes that followed Sir Roy Griffith's report into community care (Griffiths, 1988) have been aimed at the structures of the relationship between government and the bureaucracy and, through the purchaser–provider split, use market mechanisms rather than professional judgement as the means for rationing services and keeping costs down.

What is of relevance to the analysis of disability and social work is to recognise that the reorganisation of welfare following the 1990 Act was not simply an institutional one, but that it was intended to centralise control in the hands of politicians. Community care plans of local authorities and strict controls over the size and use of budgets were the mechanisms through which this control would be directly exercised while the disciplines of the market would control the actions of individual practitioners and managers. The question is, therefore, to what extent this has been or may be conducive to the development of a social work practice based on the social model of disability.

Some writers (for example Le Grand and Bartlett, 1993) have argued that these changes are necessary in order that the business of welfare can be conducted efficiently and equitably, but their analysis starts from traditional or individual-model assumptions about the causes of social need. Others such as Holman are very clear that a system based upon the ideologies of the New Right has failed and will continue to do so:

> New Right policies have failed to revive the economy. On the contrary, they have slowed the growth rate, lengthened the dole queues and deepened poverty. By exalting the free market and private ownership they have, despite their claims, restricted the choices of many and weakened democracy. Above all, they have made a god out of Mamon so that personal gain and material selfishness are regarded as virtues while the compassion for the disadvantaged and a readiness to share goods and power are sneered at as weaknesses. (Holman, 1993:26)

This argument suggests that in order for the organisation of welfare to support the practice of social work within a social model analysis of disability, there would need to be a fundamental change to the ideologies that now inform the structures of welfare. However, it would appear that the Labour government are considering the reinforcement of this ideology with their reported consideration for curtailing the Disability Living Allowance and replacing it with services provided by local authorities. This would represent a return to the administrative models of Poor Law and would be unlikely to achieve anything more than the increased institutionalisation and disablement of people with impairments. While their eventual policy is undecided at the time of writing, this proposition would follow the principles of their reductions to single-parent benefits, replacing it with child care provision to enable people to work. It would also be in line with previous Labour governments' attempts in 1948 and 1970 to provide enabling services rather than enabling resources.

While there are no radical changes to the ideology informing the welfare policies of any political party, the most promising development that has taken place is the passing of the Community Care (Direct Payments) Act 1996 which was discussed in Chapter 5. This Act is significant because, although it exploits the method of the market for the provision of care, it has the potential to shift the control and power over the purchase of services from local authorities to disabled people. Within this structure there may be the potential for social workers to practice from a social-model understanding of disability. The social work task will remain one of assessing need, but rather than then purchasing or providing services the local authority will be able to make payments of money equivalent to the cost of those services so that the disabled person is able to purchase their own personal assistance. Inevitably this will affect the relationship between the helped and helper, as the latter will be an employee not a carer, and in the long term this has the potential to change the ways in which society views the 'helped' as dependent.

However, while the potential for change exists, it remains dependent upon the local authority's assessment of need and there are some barriers to this being conducted within a social model of disability. First, the tendency to require that disabled people have to come to terms with their impairment and disability before they can be successfully helped places a precondition on the assessment of need which reinforces normative assumptions about disability based upon an individual model. This problem was integral to the analysis that led CCETSW to assert that the self-assessment of need is essential to good social work practice (Stevens, 1991). Second, the continued emphasis on budgets may limit the extent to which local authorities are prepared to relinquish their control in the determination of individual need, and self-assessment requires a partnership between social workers and disabled people which threatens that control. Furthermore, social workers may be motivated to hold onto the assessment role in a non-participatory way as it is the one thing that they retained when they were redeployed as care managers within the new welfare market. While the Barclay report may have placed an emphasis on social care planning, community social work and counselling, for many social workers in local authorities their roles and tasks have become one of social care administration, and a profession under threat may not be willing or able to assist others who are attempting to empower themselves.

Hence there are organisational pressures, embedded in the structures of the welfare system which will tend to prevent social work practice from developing the radical approach that is necessary for working within a social model of disability, but there are also professional reasons for social workers to resist them. While an entirely administrative system might overcome the problems of oppressive professionalisation, it would have less potential to stand up to the ideological inconsistencies of an individualistic social policy. The final section of this chapter therefore considers the strategies that social workers may need to employ in order to practise as professionals with disabled people in their struggle to remove disabling barriers.

Some strategies for social work

Professionalism within social work holds the potential for an anti-oppressive practice but this is dependent upon the ideologies that inform it. A profession built upon an expertise model such as medicine or law, which ignores the voices and experiences of those people they purport to serve, will do little to change the unequal and debilitating power relationships between the welfare state and disabled people. Neither will codes of ethics based upon individualistic ideologies help to achieve progress in the struggle against social barriers as they tend to value people despite, rather than because of, their difference. What is required is a form of professionalism that is capable of asserting itself in the face of oppressive social policies, but which does so with disabled people rather than for them. A social work profession that might achieve this would need several new features to its curriculum. The five that follow are not an exhaustive list though they are important.

- First, some form of disability equality training would need to be integral to the education of social workers. This is essential because of the depth to which negative assumptions about dependency and impairment are embedded in the culture of our society. Anti-disablist social work cannot be taught from text books alone as the hegemony of the individual model prevents even those who are aware of oppression from developing a full understanding of what is involved. This was seen in the debate concerning carers in Chapter 5 and the proposition that institutional care would provide a non-sexist solution to the problem of dependency (Finch, 1984). The construction of such an argument arises from an awareness and politicisation of the oppression of women, and while such theorising might be transferred to other issues such as racism or homophobia, the dominance of the individual model of disability prevents even the most politically aware people from transferring their understanding to the oppression of people with impairments. The struggle against disablism is not one of simply asserting equal rights but of challenging basic concepts of normality. As one activist put it:

> I think that the challenge that it makes to the rest of society is absolutely fundamental. I just think it's extraordinary the changes that it's trying to bring about. The whole way that people think about themselves and about their impairment. These things are very, very significant and they are changing society very fundamentally. (Jenny Morris in Campbell and Oliver, 1996:139)

In terms of the social work curriculum such an awareness-raising exercise would not simply be aimed at the individual level of practitioners and students, but at the cultural assumptions that inform CCETSW's design of the syllabus for the Diploma in Social Work. The focus on normality and deviancy through the inclusion of the study of human growth and development within this syllabus typifies the way in which, despite their exhortation of the social model within the context of anti-discriminatory practice, social work education is still dominated by the theories based on the individual model of disability.

- Second, although awareness is essential, it is insufficient to bring about an informed social work practice. What is also required is that social workers have a knowledge of the social model of disability that will inform their actions as practitioners and managers within a welfare system that itself has been seen to be oppressive. As an example, take the position of a social worker who is seeking to provide a package of care to a disabled person to enable them to live independently. If the cost of this service exceeds the price of a place in a nursing home then it is common practice in many local authorities for the budget holder to refuse the service and offer only to pay for the nursing placement, particularly if the disabled person is over 65 years of age. As care is viewed in a functional way, the nursing home is seen to provide all that the person requires and their wish to live in their own home is interpreted as an unreasonable demand on the community care budget. A simple argument of rights or choice is unlikely to have much impact.

  What the social worker needs is to be able to analyse the models that inform the budget holder's decision and to show how it is misinformed. In other words, it is necessary to first show how the decision is the result of an individual-model analysis of need in the particular case, and then to show why this model does not stand up to critical scrutiny. This will require a good knowledge of the psychological, sociological and economic origins of disability to a level that would allow the social-model analysis to be applied in a multitude of situations.

  There is no guarantee that budget holders are going to react favourably to such criticisms and be immediately converted to an alternative analysis of disability, but it is essential to undermine their assertion that welfare should respond to impairment and to demonstrate that this is inefficient, ineffective and uneconomic by arguing that the outcomes in terms of disablement are unchanged or worsened by such an approach. It is necessary to continuously assert the value of directing welfare spending at reducing disability if more appropriate outcome criteria are to be eventually adopted.

- Third, the most common area in which disputes will arise is that of assessment of need. While local authorities retain the right to determine the needs of individuals there will always be a level of conflict over the interpretation and assessment of need. This was discussed in detail in Chapter 3 and various strategies for practitioners to undertake assessments within a social model were proposed. At the core of these were the issues of empowerment and self-assessment. However, what may also be required is that social workers adopt a position of 'determined advocacy' in relation to supporting the rights of individual disabled people to participate and to define their own needs.

This is the position that was recommended by BASW when the Social Fund was first introduced and social workers were expected to participate in determining priorities for what had previously been a series of single payments under the supplementary benefits system and available as of right in certain circumstances. Determined advocacy implies not making judgements about whether the request, or in this case the self-assessment of need, is correct to some normative criteria, but to advocate for that assessment without reservation. This is not to relinquish any form of professional judgement or involvement with the individual concerned as the advice and experience of the social worker may be of immense value in helping disabled people develop strategies in their self-assessment. Rather, it is to ensure that the social work role is not to act as yet another barrier to independent living – it is to enable rather than disable.

- Fourth is the role of counselling in social work practice with disabled people. This is a matter that social workers often dispute as to whether it is part of their task, with some viewing it as the only therapeutic skill that they can genuinely possess while others consider it to be a specialist activity and not part of the administration of welfare. There are good arguments for both positions.

Those who support the practice of counselling would suggest that social work is not simply a matter of administrating the delivery of material and personal services, but one of helping people who are failing to realise their potential within the social sphere of their lives to do so. As such, counselling becomes a useful skill to either raise the consciousness of individuals or, in a less radical manner, to help people understand the meanings of their own actions.

A counter to this argument is that because of the position that social workers occupy within the power structures of the welfare system, it would be wrong to employ skills that may blur the transparency with which their actions should be conducted if they are to enable the full participation of their clients. This view may see counselling as a manipulative process or simply as a matter that should be kept quite separate from the provision of social services.

To some extent both these arguments are conducted within an individual model of understanding of disability in which counselling is used to either help people come to terms with their impairment, or not if it is seen as an inadequate response to the request for material help. From the perspective of the social model, what is required is to evaluate the usefulness of counselling in the struggle to remove disabling barriers. One piece of research into what might constitute counselling in a social model of practice concluded that:

> The focus of counselling physically disabled people seems to be one of very consciously giving control back to the client or enabling the client to empower themselves through practical, emotional and social means. This is found to be necessary as many disabled people have had difficult and often painful experiences at the hands of the medical and allied professions or in their families or in interactions with the public at large. Due to their circumstances they have had to rely on others for their practical needs and sometimes the 'professionals' or family members have taken over the decision making for the disabled person. The result of feeling out of control, in a practical sense, has led to emotional difficulties for some disabled people. The emotional cost for them of not feeling empowered is having low self esteem, low self confidence and a feeling of worthlessness. (Oliver, J., 1995:275)

Thus counselling can play a useful and necessary role in countering the impact of many of the disabling barriers that people with impairments face. While it would certainly be right for social workers to refuse to counsel people with the aim of getting them to accept the non-provision of material resources, it would be wrong to reject counselling *per se*.

• Fifth, there is a need to rediscover the role of community social work within community care. The onset of care management has had the effect of neutralising social work as a radical activity. The development of procedures and regulations for the provision of services along with the limitation of the legitimate role of social work to this instrumental activity has curtailed many of the roles of social workers that were previously undisputed. Social work within local authorities tends to be viewed as a purely administrative process and one that might legitimately be undertaken by people with some other form of training. However, this would be to accept that the current organisation of disability services and of welfare in general is appropriate and that there is no need for it to be challenged from within the system.

Community social work has always meant working within and with communities to assist them to realise greater benefits from the welfare state, and it is to these roles of advocacy and development that social work must return. The struggle against disability is a collective one as the solutions are social rather than individual. If social work is to be an effective ally to the struggle and to use its influence within the welfare state to alter and modify disability policies, it must do so from a position that is informed by its work with collective organisations of disabled people.

Individual disabled people who are isolated from these developments are quite likely to be in touch with social workers who can help by making them aware of the collective nature of their problems. Social workers can also help groups of disabled people to be heard in preference to the traditional organisations *for* the disabled that have established access to social service managements.

It is impossible and would be quite wrong to attempt to reproduce the instrumentalism of care management by giving a list of social work tasks that flow from an acceptance of the social model of disability, and the issues that have been highlighted here are the most obvious and perhaps most urgent that need to be addressed by the social work establishment – its professional bodies, education providers and principal employers. It is only by examining and re-examining the implications of the social-model analysis for the structures of social policy, the management of the welfare system and the actual practice of social work that social workers will be able to formulate a means of working which is meaningful and useful for disabled people.

* * *

Conclusion

The first edition of this book was written in the hope that the social model of disability would provide a useful basis for constructing an effective social work practice with disabled people. In the subsequent 15 years, economic and political changes coupled with a less than inspired professional leadership of the social work profession has meant that many of earlier hopes have not materialised. However, the emergence of a strong and committed movement of disabled people based upon the social model of disability has meant that an enabling professional practice remains firmly on the agenda.

In this second edition, we have attempted to reconstruct this professional practice in the light of these changing economic and political circumstances. This is because we remain committed to the idea of an enabling welfare state based upon empowering professional practice. We hope that this book will be a vehicle for such a reconstruction because if we fail in this task, not only will there be no third edition of this book in 15 years time, but the idea and practice of an enabling and empowering welfare state will itself be dead and there will be no professional practice to reconstruct.

References

Abberley, P. (1992) 'Counting Us Out: A Discussion of the OPCS Disability Surveys', *Disability, Handicap and Society*, vol. 9, no. 2, pp. 139–55.

Aboville, E. d' (1991) 'Social Work in an Organisation of Disabled People', in M. Oliver (ed.), *Social Work, Disabled People and Disabling Environments*, London: Jessica Kingsley.

Abrams, P. (1978) 'Community Care: Some Research Problems and Priorities', in J. Barnes and N. Connelly (eds), *Social Care Research*, London: Bedford Square Press.

ACE (1996) *Special Education Handbook: The Law on Children with Special Needs*, London: Advisory Centre for Education.

Albrecht, G. L. (ed.) (1976) *The Sociology of Physical Disability and Rehabilitation*, University of Pittsburgh Press.

Albrecht, G. and Levy, J. (1981) 'Constructing Disabilities as Social Problems', in G. Albrecht (ed.), *Cross National Rehabilitation Policies: A Sociological Perspective*, Beverly Hills: Sage.

Aldersea, P. (1996) *National Prosthetic and Wheelchair Service Report*, London: College of Occupational Therapy.

Aldridge, J. and Becker, S. (1996) 'Disability Rights and the Denial of Young Carers: The Dangers of Zero-Sum Arguments', *Critical Social Policy*, vol. 16 (3), pp. 55–76.

Ambrose, I. (1997) *Lifetime Homes in Europe and the UK: European Legislation and Good Practice for Ensuring Accessibility of Domestic Dwellings*, Housing Research Findings, York: Joseph Rowntree Foundation.

Audit Commission (1986) *Making a Reality of Community Care*, London: HMSO.

Avery, D. (1997) Message to <disability-research@mailbase.ac.uk> discussion group, RE: age onset of disability, 9 June.

Bailey, R. and Lee, P. (eds) (1982) *Theory and Practice in Social Work*, Oxford: Blackwell.

Baird, P. (1980) 'The Last Word', *Social Work Today*, 19 August.

Baistow, K. (1995) 'Liberation and Regulation? Some Paradoxes of Empowerment', *Critical Social Policy*, issue 42, pp. 34–46.

Barclay Committee (1982) *Social Workers: Their Role and Tasks*, London: Bedford Square Press.

Barnes, C. (1991) *Disabled People in Britain and Discrimination. A Case for Anti-Discrimination Legislation*, London: Hurst & Co.

Barnes, C. (1997) 'A Legacy of Oppression: A History of Disability in Western Culture', in L. Barton and M. Oliver (eds), *Disability Studies: Past, Present and Future*, Leeds: The Disability Press.

Barnes, C. and Oliver, M. (1995) 'Disability Rights: Rhetoric and Reality in the UK', *Disability and Society*, vol. 10, no. 1, pp. 111–16.

185

Barton, R. (1959) *Institutional Neurosis*, London: John Wright.

Battye, L. (1966) 'The Chatterley Syndrome', in P. Hunt (ed.), *Stigma*, London: Geoffrey Chapman.

Beardshaw, V. (1993) 'Conductive Education: A Rejoinder', in J. Swain, V. Finkelstein, S. French and M. Oliver (eds), *Disabling Barriers – Enabling Environments*, London: Sage.

Becker, H. (1963) *Outsiders: Studies in the Sociology of Deviance*, New York: Free Press.

Begum, N. Hill, M. and Stevens, A. (eds) (1994) *Reflections: The Views of Black Disabled People on their Lives and on Community Care*, London: CCETSW.

Bell, L. and Klemz, A. (1981) *Physical Handicap*, Cambridge: Woodhead-Faulkner.

Berger, R. (1988) 'Helping Clients Survive a Loss', *Social Work Today*, vol. 19, no. 34, pp. 14–17.

Blaug, R. (1995) 'Distortion of the Face to Face: Communicative Reason and Social Work Practice', *British Journal of Social Work*, vol. 25, no. 4, pp. 423–39.

Blaxter, M. (1980) *The Meaning of Disability*, 2nd edn, London: Heinemann.

Bloomfield, R. (1976) *Younger Chronic Sick Units: A Survey and Critique*, unpublished paper.

Bone, M. and Meltzer, H. (1989) *The Prevalence of Disability Among Children*, London: HMSO.

Bonnett, D. (1996) *Incorporating Lifetime Homes Standards into Modernisation Programmes*, Housing Research Findings, York: Joseph Rowntree Foundation.

Booth, T. (1981) 'Demystifying Integration', in W. Swann (ed.), *The Practice of Special Education*, Oxford: Blackwell in association with the Open University Press.

Booth, T. (1992) *Reasons for Admission to Part iii Residential Homes*, London: National Council of Domiciliary Care Services.

Boswell, D. M. and Wingrove, J. M. (eds) (1974) *The Handicapped Person in the Community*, London: Tavistock.

Bradshaw, J. (1980) *The Handicapped Child and His Family. The Family Fund: An Initiative in Social Policy*, London: Routledge & Kegan Paul.

Braye, S. and Preston-Shoot, M. (1997) *Practising Social Work Law*, 2nd edn, Basingstoke: Macmillan.

Brechin, A., Liddiard, P. and Swain, J. (eds) (1981) *Handicap in a Social World*, London: Hodder & Stoughton.

Brechin, A. and Liddiard, P. (1981) *Look at it this Way: New Perspectives in Rehabilitation*, London: Hodder & Stoughton.

Brewer, C. and Lait, J. (1980) *Can Social Work Survive?* London: Temple Smith.

British Association of Social Workers (BASW) (1982) *Guidelines for Social Work with the Disabled*, draft paper, London: BASW.

British Association of Social Workers (BASW) (1990) *Managing Care: The Social Work Task*, Birmingham: BASW.

Brown, H. and Craft, A. (eds) (1989) *Thinking the Unthinkable: Papers on Sexual Abuse and People with Learning Difficulties*, London: Family Planning Association.

Buckle, J. (1971) *Work and Housing of Impaired People in Great Britain*, London: HMSO.

Burgess, P. (1982) 'In Benefit', *Community Care*, 1 July 1982.

Burgess, P. (1996) 'Social Security', *Research Matters*, April–October 1996, pp. 22–4.

Bury, M. (1996) 'Defining and Researching Disability: Challenges and Responses', in C. Barnes and G. Mercer (eds), *Exploring the Divide: Illness and Disability*, Leeds: The Disability Press.

Campbell, J. (1997) 'Implementing Direct Payments: Towards the Next Millennium', in S. Balloch and N. Connelly (eds), *Buying and Selling Social Care*, London: National Institute for Social Work.

Campbell, J. and Oliver, M. (eds) (1996) *Disability Politics*, London: Routledge.

Carroll, T. J. (1961) *Blindness – What it Is, What it Does, and How to Live with It*, Boston: Little, Brown.

Carver, V. (1982) *The Individual Behind the Statistics*, Milton Keynes: Open University Press.

Casserly, J. and Clark, B. (1978) *A Welfare Rights Approach to the Chronically Sick and Disabled*, Strathclyde Regional Council.

Central Council for Education and Training in Social Work (CCETSW) (1974) *Social Work: People with Handicaps Need Better Trained Workers*, London: CCETSW.

Clark, F. le Gros (1969) *Blinded in War: A Model for the Welfare of all Handicapped People*, Herts: Wayland.

Cobbold, C. (1997) *A Cost Benefit Analysis of Lifetime Homes*, York: Joseph Rowntree Foundation.

Cook, J. and Mitchell, P. (1982) *Putting Teeth in the Act: A History of Attempts to Enforce the Provisions of Section 2 of the Chronically Sick and Disabled Persons Act 1970*, London: RADAR.

Corrigan, P. and Leonard, P. (1979) *Social Work Practice under Capitalism*, London: Macmillan.

Creek, G., Moore, M., Oliver, M., Salisbury, V., Silver, J. and Zarb, G. (1987) *The Social Implication of Spinal Cord Injury*, London: Thames Polytechnic.

Croft, S. (1986) 'Women, Caring and the Recasting of Need – A Feminist Reappraisal', *Critical Social Policy*, issue 16, pp. 23–39.

Crow, L. (1996) 'Including All of Our Lives: Renewing the Social Model of Disability', in C. Barnes and G. Mercer (eds), *Exploring the Divide: Illness and Disability*, Leeds: The Disability Press.

Cypher, J. (ed.) (1979) *Seebohm Across Three Decades*, London: BASW.

Dalley, G. (1996) *Ideologies of Caring*, Basingstoke: Macmillan.

Daly, M. and Noble, M. (1996) 'The Reach of Disability Benefits:

An Examination of the Disability Living Allowance', *Journal of Social Welfare and Family Law*, vol. 18 (1), pp. 37–51.

Dartington, T., Miller, E. and Gwynne, G. (1981) *A Life Together*, London: Tavistock.

Davis, K. (1981) '28–38 Grove Road: Accommodation and Care in a Community Setting', in A. Brechin, P. Liddiard and J. Swain (eds), *Handicap in a Social World*, London: Hodder & Stoughton.

Davis K. and Woodward, J. (1981) 'DIAL UK: Development of the National Association of Disablement Information and Advice Services', in A. Brechin, P. Liddiard and J. Swain (eds) *Handicap in a Social World*, London: Hodder & Stoughton.

Department of Health and Social Security (1968) *Report of the Committee on Local Authority and Allied Social Services*, Seebohm Report, London: HMSO.

Department of Health and Social Security (1976) *The Way Forward: Priorities for Health and Personal Social Services in England*, London: HMSO.

Department of Health and Social Security (1981) *Care in Action*, London: HMSO.

Department of Health (1989) *Caring for People – Community Care in the Next Decade and Beyond*, London: HMSO.

Department of Health (1996) *Statistical Bulletin: Residential Accommodation Statistics 1996*, London: Department of Health.

Despouy, L. (1993) *Human Rights and Disability*, New York: United Nations Economic and Social Council.

Dickinson, M. (1977) 'Rehabilitating the Traumatically Disabled Adult', *Social Work Today*, vol. 8, no. 28.

Douglas, J. (ed.) (1970) *Deviance and Respectability: The Social Construction of Moral Meanings*, New York: BASK Books.

Doyal, L. (1980) *The Political Economy of Health*, London: Pluto Press.

Doyal, L. and Gough, I. (1991) *A Theory of Human Need*, Basingstoke: Macmillan.

Ellis, K. (1993) *Squaring the Circle: User and Carer Participation in Needs Assessment*, York: Joseph Rowntree Foundation.

Employment Department Group (1990) *Employment and Training for People with Disabilities*, London: Employment Department Group.

Equal Opportunities Commission (1982) *Caring for the Elderly and Handicapped*, London: Equal Opportunities Commission.

Family Policies Study Centre (1997) *A Guide to Family Issues: Family Briefing Paper 2*, London: Family Policies Study Centre.

Feidler, B. (1988) *Living Options Lottery*, London: King's Fund Centre.

Finch, J. (1984) 'Community Care: Developing Non-Sexist Alternatives', *Critical Social Policy*, issue 9, pp. 6–18.

Finkelstein, V. (1980) *Attitudes and Disabled People: Issues for Discussion*, New York: World Rehabilitation Fund.

Finkelstein, V. (1981) *Disability and Professional Attitudes*, Sevenoaks: NAIDEX Convention.

Finkelstein, V. (1991) 'Disability: An Administrative Challenge? (The

Health and Welfare Heritage)', in M. Oliver (ed.), *Social Work, Disabled People and Disabling Environments*, London: Jessica Kingsley.

Finkelstein, V. and Stuart, O. (1996) 'Developing New Services', in G. Hales (ed.), *Beyond Disability*, London: Sage.

Finlay, B. (1978) *Housing and Disability: A Report on the Housing Needs of Physically Handicapped People in Rochdale*, Rochdale Voluntary Action.

Fitzgerald, R. G. (1970) 'Reaction to Blindness: An Exploratory Study of Adults', *Archives of General Psychiatry*, vol. 22, April, Chicago: American Medical Association.

Fox, A. M. (1974) *They Get This Training But They Don't Really Know How You Feel*, London: RADAR.

Freire, P. (1972) *Pedagogy of the Oppressed*, Harmondsworth: Penguin.

Froggatt, A. (1990) *Family Work with Elderly People*, Basingstoke: Macmillan.

Froggett, L. and Sapey, B. (1997) 'Communication, Culture and Competence in Social Work Education', *Social Work Education*, vol. 16, no. 1, pp. 41–53.

Glastonbury B (1995) 'Risk, Information Technology and Social Care', *New Technology in the Human Services*, vol. 8, no. 3, pp. 2–10.

Glendinning, C. (1981) *Resource Worker Project: Final Report*, Social Policy Research Unit, University of York.

Goffman, E. (1961) *Asylums*, New York: Doubleday.

Goffman, E. (1963) *Stigma: Some Notes on the Management of Spoiled Identity*, Englewood Cliffs, N.J.: Prentice-Hall.

Goldberg, M. and Warburton, C. (1979) *Ends and Means in Social Work*, London: Allen & Unwin.

Goldsmith, S. (1976) *Designing for the Disabled*, 3rd edn, London: Royal Institute of British Architects.

Gooding, C. (1996) *Blackstone's Guide to the Disability Discrimination Act 1995*, London: Blackstone Press.

Griffiths, Sir, R. (1988) *Community Care: Agenda for Action*, London: HMSO.

Groce, N. (1985) *Everyone Here Spoke Sign Language: Hereditary Deafness on Martha's Vineyard*, London: Harvard University Press.

Grover, R. and Gladstone, G. (1982) *Disabled People – A Right to Work?* London: Bedford Square Press.

Halliburton, P. and Quelch, K. (1981) *Get Help: A Guide for Social Workers to the Management of Illness in the Community*, London: Tavistock.

Hanks, J. and Hanks, L. (1980) 'The Physically Handicapped in Certain Non-occidental Societies', in W. Phillips and J. Rosenberg (eds), *Social Scientists and the Physically Handicapped*, London: Arno Press.

Hanvey, C. (1981) *Social Work with Mentally Handicapped People*, London: Heinemann.

Harris, A. (1971) *Handicapped and Impaired in Great Britain*, London: HMSO.

Harris, J. (1995) *The Cultural Meaning of Deafness*, Aldershot: Avebury.

Harris, J. (1997) *Deafness and the Hearing*, Birmingham: Venture Press.
Harris, J., Sapey, B. and Stewart, J. (1997) *Wheelchair Housing and the Estimation of Need*, Preston: University of Central Lancashire/ National Wheelchair Housing Association Group.
Hatch, S. (1980) *Outside the State*, London: Croom Helm.
Holdsworth, L. (1991) *Empowerment Social Work with Physically Disabled People*, Norwich: Social Work Monographs.
Holman, B. (1993) *A New Deal for Social Welfare*, Oxford: Lion.
Howe, D. (1987) *An Introduction to Social Work Theory*, Aldershot: Wildwood House.
Hughes, B. (1995) *Older People and Community Care: Critical Theory and Practice*, Buckingham: Open University Press.
Hunt, P. (1981) 'Settling Accounts with the Parasite People: a Critique of *A Life Apart* by Miller and Gwynne', *Disability Challenge*, no. 1, UPIAS.
Ibbotson, J. (1975) 'Psychological Effects of Physical Disability', *Occupational Therapy*, January.
Illich, I. (1975) *Medical Nemesis: The Expropriation of Health*, London: Marion Boyars.
Inkeles, A. (1964) *What is Sociology?* Englewood Cliffs, NJ: Prentice-Hall.
Jacques, M. (1997) 'Les Enfants de Marx et de Coca-Cola', *New Statesman*, 28 November, pp. 34–6.
Jay Report (1979) *Report of the Committee of Enquiry into Mental Handicap Nursing and Care*, London: HMSO.
Jones, C. (1994) *Dangerous Times for British Social Work Education*. A paper to the 27th Congress of the International Association of Schools of Social Work. Amsterdam.
Keeble, U. (1979) *Aids and Adaptations*, London: Bedford Square Press.
Keith, L. and Morris, J. (1995) 'Easy Targets: A Disability Rights Perspective on the "Children as Carers" Debate', *Critical Social Policy*, vol. 15 (2/3), pp. 36–57.
Kelly, L. (1992) 'The Connections between Disability and Child Abuse: A Review of the Research Evidence', *Child Abuse Review*, vol. 1(3), pp. 157–67.
Kennedy, M. (1989) 'The Abuse of Deaf Children', *Child Abuse Review*, vol. 3(1), pp. 3–7.
Knight, R. and Warren, M. (1978) *Physically Handicapped People Living at Home: A Study of Numbers and Needs*, London: HMSO.
Kuhn, T. (1962) *The Structure of Scientific Revolutions*, Chicago: University of Chicago Press.
Langan, M. (1990) 'Community Care in the 1990s: The Community Care White Paper: "Caring for People"', *Critical Social Policy*, issue 29, pp. 58–70.
Large, P. (1981) *Enabling the Disabled: Voluntary Initiative and the Autonomy of Disabled People*, paper given to Royal College of Physicians, 1 October.
Laurie, L. (ed.) (1991) *Building Our Lives: Housing, Independent Living and Disabled People*, London: Shelter.

Leat, D. (1988) 'Residential Care for Younger Physically Disabled Adults', in I. Sinclair (ed.), *Residential Care: The Research Reviewed*, London: HMSO.

Le Grand, J. and Bartlett, W. (eds) (1993) *Quasi-Markets and Social Policy*, Basingstoke: Macmillan.

Lemert, E. (1967) *Human Deviance, Social Problems and Social Control*, Englewood Cliffs, NJ: Prentice-Hall.

Lenny, J. (1993) 'Do Disabled People Need Counselling?' in J. Swain, V. Finkelstein, S. French and M. Oliver (eds), *Disabling Barriers – Enabling Environments*, London: Sage.

Leonard, P. (1966) 'The Challenge of Primary Prevention', *Social Work Today*, 6 October.

Lonsdale, G., Elfer, P. and Ballard, R. (1979) *Children, Grief and Social Work*, Oxford: Blackwell.

MacFarlane, A. (1994) 'On Becoming an Older Disabled Woman', *Disability and Society*, vol. 9, no. 2, pp. 255–6.

Marchant, R. and Page, M. (1992) *Bridging the Gap*, London: National Society for the Prevention of Cruelty to Children.

Marshall, M. (1996) *'I Can't Place this Place at All.' Working with People with Dementia and their Carers*, Birmingham: Venture Press.

Marshall, M. and Dixon, M. (1996) *Social Work with Old People*, 3rd edn, Basingstoke: Macmillan.

Martin, J., Meltzer, H. and Elliot, D. (1988) *The Prevalence Of Disability among Adults*, London: HMSO.

Martin, J., White, A. and Meltzer, H. (1989) *Disabled Adults: Services, Transport and Employment*, London: HMSO.

McKnight, J. (1981) 'Professionalised Service and Disabled Help', in A. Brechin, P. Liddiard and J. Swain (eds), *Handicap in a Social World*, London: Hodder & Stoughton.

Merton, R. (1957) *Social Theory and Social Structure*, New York: Free Press.

Meteyard, B. (1992) *Assessment of Need: The OPAL Package*, London: NALGO Education.

Middleton, L. (1992) *Children First: Working with Children and Disability*, Birmingham: Venture Press.

Middleton, L. (1995) *Making a Difference: Social Work with Disabled Children*, Birmingham: Venture Press.

Middleton, L. (1997) *The Art of Assessment: Practitioners' Guide*, Birmingham: Venture Press.

Miller, E. and Gwynne, G. (1971) *A Life Apart*, London: Tavistock.

Morris, J. (ed.) (1989) *Able Lives: Women's Experience of Paralysis*, London: The Women's Press.

Morris, J. (1990) *Freedom to Lose: Housing Policy and People with Disabilities*, London: Shelter.

Morris, J. (1991) *Pride Against Prejudice*, London: Women's Press.

Morris, J. (1992) *Disabled Lives: Many Voices, One Message*, London: BBC Education.

Morris, J. (1993) *Community Care or Independent Living*, York: Joseph Rowntree Foundation.

Morris, J. (1997a) *Community Care: Working in Partnership with Service Users*, Birmingham: Venture Press.

Morris, J. (1997b) 'Gone Missing? Disabled Children Living Away from their Families', *Disability and Society*, vol. 12, no. 2, pp. 241–58.

Musgrove, F. (1977) *Margins of the Mind*, London: Methuen.

Nissel, M. and Bonnerjea, L. (1982) *Family Care of the Handicapped Elderly: Who Pays?* London: Policy Studies Institute.

North Surrey CHC (1978) *Care and Facilities for the Younger Disabled*, unpublished paper.

Oliver, J. (1982) 'Community Care: Who Pays?', *New Society*, 24 March.

Oliver, J. (1995) 'Counselling Disabled People: A Counsellor's Perspective', *Disability and Society*, vol. 10, no. 3, pp. 261–79.

Oliver, M. (1982) *Disablement in Society*, Milton Keynes: Open University Press.

Oliver, M. (1983) *Social Work with Disabled People*, Basingstoke: Macmillan.

Oliver, M. (1990) *The Politics of Disablement*, Basingstoke: Macmillan.

Oliver, M. (ed) (1991) *Social Work, Disabled People and Disabling Environments*, London: Jessica Kingsley.

Oliver, M. (1993) 'Conductive Education: If It Wasn't so Sad It Would be Funny', in J. Swain, V. Finkelstein, S. French and M. Oliver (eds), *Disabling Barriers – Enabling Environments*, London: Sage.

Oliver, M. (1996) *Understanding Disability: From Theory to Practice*, Basingstoke: Macmillan.

Oliver, M. and Zarb, G. (1992) *Greenwich Personal Assistance Schemes: An Evaluation*, London: Greenwich Association of Disabled People.

Owen, T. (1981) 'How Remploy's Survey helped Barclay', *Community Care*, 12 November.

Parsloe, P. and Stevenson, O. (1978) *Social Services Teams: The Practitioners' View*, London: HMSO.

Payne, C. (1978) 'Working with Groups in the Residential Setting', in N. McCaughan (ed.), *Groupwork: Learning and Practice*, London: Allen & Unwin.

Phelan, P. (1979) 'The Last Word', *Social Work Today*, vol. 10.

Phillips, H. and Glendinning, C. (1981) *Who Benefits?* London: The Disability Alliance.

Pitkeathley, J. (1996) 'Carers', *Research Matters*, April–October 1996, pp. 58–60.

Powles, J. (1973) 'On the Limitations of Modern Medicine', *Science, Medicine and Man*, vol. 1.

Ratzka, A. (1991) 'The Swedish Experience', in L. Laurie (ed.), *Building Our Lives: Housing, Independent Living and Disabled People*, London: Shelter.

Rioux, M., Crawford, M. and Bach, M. (1997) 'Uncovering the Shape of Violence: A Research Methodology Rooted in the Experience of People with Disabilities', in C. Barnes and G. Mercer (eds), *Doing Disability Research*, Leeds: The Disability Press.

Robinson, D. and Henry, S. (1977) *Self-Help and Health*, London: Martin Robertson.

Robinson, T. (1978) *In Worlds Apart: Professionals and their Clients in the Welfare State*, London: Bedford Square Press.

Roith, A. (1974) 'The Myth of Parental Attitudes', in D. M. Boswell and J. M. Wingrove (eds), *The Handicapped Person in the Community*, London: Tavistock.

Rowan, P. (1980) *What Sort of Life?* Windsor: NFER Publishing.

Rowlings, C. (1981) *Social Work with Elderly People*, London: Allen & Unwin.

Royal Commission on the National Health Service (1979) *Report*, London: HMSO.

Ryan, J. and Thomas, F. (1980) *The Politics of Mental Handicap*, Harmondsworth: Penguin.

Safilios-Rothschild, C. (1970) *The Sociology and Social Psychology of Disability and Rehabilitation*, New York: Random House.

Sainsbury, S. (1970) *Registered as Disabled*, Occasional Papers on Social Administration, no. 35, London: Bell.

Sapey, B. (1993) 'Community Care: Reinforcing the Dependency of Disabled People', *Applied Community Studies*, vol. 1, no. 3, pp. 21–9.

Sapey, B. (1995) 'Disabling Homes: A Study of the Housing Needs of Disabled People in Cornwall', *Disability and Society*, vol. 10, no. 1, pp. 71–85.

Sapey, B. and Hewitt, N. (1991) 'The Changing Context of Social Work Practice', in M. Oliver (ed.), *Social Work, Disabled People and Disabling Barriers*, London: Jessica Kingsley.

Satyamurti, C. (1981) *Occupational Survival*, Oxford: Blackwell.

Schorr, A. (1992) *The Personal Social Services: An Outside View*, York: Joseph Rowntree Foundation.

Scott, R. A. (1970) 'The Constructions and Conceptions of Stigma by Professional Experts', in J. Douglas (ed.), *Deviance and Respectability: The Social Construction of Moral Meanings*, New York: BASK Books.

Scrutton, S. (1989) *Counselling Older People: A Creative Response to Ageing*, London: Edward Arnold.

Selfe, L. and Stow, L. (1981) *Children with Handicaps*, London: Hodder & Stoughton.

Shakespeare, T. (1996) 'Power and Prejudice: Issues of Gender, Sexuality and Disability', in L. Barton (ed.), *Disability and Society: Emerging Issues and Insights*, London: Longman.

Shakespeare, T. (1997) 'Researching Disabled Sexuality', in C. Barnes and G. Mercer (eds), *Doing Disability Research*, Leeds: The Disability Press.

Shakespeare, T., Gillespie-Sells, K. and Davies, D. (1996) *The Sexual Politics of Disability: Untold Desires*, London: Cassell.

Shearer, A. (1981a) *Disability: Whose Handicap?* Oxford: Blackwell.

Shearer, A. (1981b) 'A Framework for Independent Living', in A. Walker and P. Townsend (eds), *Disability in Britain*, London: Martin Robertson.

Shearer, A. (1984) *Centres for Independent Living in the US and the UK – An American Viewpoint*, London: King's Fund Centre.

Silburn, R. (1983) 'Social Assistance and Social Welfare: The Legacy of the Poor Law', in P. Bean and S. MacPherson (eds), *Approaches to Welfare*, London: Routledge & Kegan Paul.

Simkins, J. and Tickner, V. (1978) *Whose Benefit?* London: RADAR.

Simpson, F. and Campbell, J. (1996) *Facilitating and Supporting Independent Living: A Guide to Setting Up a Personal Assistance Scheme*, London: Disablement Income Group.

Social Services Inspectorate and Social Work Services Group (1991a) *Care Management and Assessment: Managers Guide*, London: HMSO.

Social Services Inspectorate and Social Work Services Group (1991b) *Care Management and Assessment: Practitioners Guide*, London: HMSO.

Social Services Inspectorate (1995) *Growing Up and Moving On: Report of an SSI Project on the Transition Services for Disabled Young People*, London: HMSO.

Social Services Inspectorate (1997) *Moving on towards Independence: Second Report of an SSI Project on the Transition Services for Disabled Young People*, London: HMSO.

Stevens, A. (1991) *Disability Issues*, London: CCETSW.

Stewart, W. (1979) *The Sexual Side of Handicap*, Cambridge: Woodhead-Faulkner.

Stuart, O. (1994) 'Journey from the Margin: Black Disabled People and the Antiracist Debate', in N. Begum, M. Hill and A. Stevens (eds), *Reflections: The Views of Black Disabled People on their Lives and on Community Care*, London: CCETSW.

Stuart, O. (1995) 'Response to Mike Oliver's Review of "Reflections"', *Disability and Society*, vol. 10, no. 3, pp. 371–3.

Sutherland, A. T. (1981) *Disabled We Stand*, London: Souvenir Press.

Swain, J. (1981) *Adopting a Life-Style*, Milton Keynes: Open University Press.

Swain, J., Finkelstein, V., French, S. and Oliver, M. (eds) (1993) *Disabling Barriers – Enabling Environments*, London: Sage.

Tate, D. G., Maynard, F. and Forchheimer, M. (1992) 'Evaluation of a Medical Rehabilitation and Independent Living Programme for Persons with Spinal Cord Injury', *Journal of Rehabilitation*, vol. 58, pp. 25–8.

Taylor, D. (1977) *Physical Impairment Social Handicap*, London: Office of Health Economics.

Thompson, N. (1993) *Anti-Discriminatory Practice*, Basingstoke: Macmillan.

Tisdall, E. K. M. (1994) 'Why Not Consider Citizenship? A Critique of Post-School Transitional Models for Young Disabled People', *Disability and Society*, vol. 9, no. 1, pp. 3–18.

Tomlinson, S. (1982) *The Sociology of Special Education*, London: Routledge & Kegan Paul.

Topliss, E. (1979) *Provision for the Disabled*, 2nd edn, Oxford: Blackwell, with Martin Robertson.

Topliss, E. and Gould, B. (1981) *A Charter for the Disabled*, Oxford: Blackwell.

References

Townsend, P. (1979) *Poverty in the United Kingdom*, Har Penguin.

Trieschmann, R. B. (1980) *Spinal Cord Injuries*, Oxford: Perg. Press.

Tuckey, R. and Tuckey L. (1981) *An Ordinary Place*, Windsor: NFER-Nelson.

UPIAS (1976) *Fundamental Principles of Disability*, London: Union of Physically Impaired Against Segregation.

Walker, A. and Townsend, P. (eds) (1981) *Disability in Britain*, London: Martin Robertson.

Warnock Report (1978) *Special Educational Needs: Report of the Committee of Enquiry into the Education of Children and Young People*, London: HMSO.

Warren, M. D., Knight, R. and Warren, J. L. (1979) *Changing Capabilities and Needs of People with Handicaps*, Health Services Research Unit, University of Kent.

Weller, D. J. and Miller, P. M. (1977) 'Emotional Reactions of Patient, Family, and Staff in Acute Care Period of Spinal Cord Injury: part 2', *Social Work in Health Care*, vol. 3.

Westcott, H. (1993) *Abuse of Children and Adults with Disabilities*, London: NSPCC.

Westcott, H. and Cross, M. (1995) *This Far and No Further: Towards Ending the Abuse of Disabled Children*, Birmingham: Venture Press.

Wilding, P. (1982) *Professional Power and Social Welfare*, London: Routledge & Kegan Paul.

Wilkin, D. (1979) *Caring for the Mentally Handicapped Child*, London: Croom Helm.

Willis, M. (1995) 'Customer Expectations of Service Quality at Community Team Offices', *Social Services Research*, no. 4, pp. 57–67.

World Health Organisation (1980) *International Classification of Impairments, Disabilities and Handicaps*, Geneva: WHO.

Young, M. and Willmott, P. (1973) *The Symmetrical Family*, Harmondsworth: Penguin.

Ypren, T. A. van (1996) 'On Coding and Classification in Social Welfare', *New Technology in Human Services*, vol. 9, no. 3 pp. 3–10.

Zarb, G. (1991) 'Creating a Supportive Environment: Meeting the Needs of People who are Ageing with a Disability', in M. Oliver (ed.), *Social Work, Disabled People and Disabling Environments*, London: Jessica Kingsley.

Zarb, G. (1993) 'The Dual Experience of Ageing with a Disability', in J. Swain, V Finkelstein, S. French and M. Oliver (eds), *Disabling Barriers – Enabling Environments*, London: Sage.

Zarb, G. and Nadash, P. (1994) *Cashing in on Independence*, London: Policy Studies Institute for the British Council of Disabled People.

Zarb, G., Oliver, M. and Silver, J. (1990) *Ageing with Spinal Cord Injury: The Right to a Supportive Environment?* London: Thames Polytechnic/Spinal Injuries Association.

Index